AF765194

Palgrave Socio-Legal Studies

Series Editor
Dave Cowan
School of Law
University of Cardiff
Cardiff, UK

Editorial Board
Dame Hazel Genn
University College London
London, UK

Fiona Haines
School of Social & Political Sciences
University of Melbourne
Melbourne, Australia

Herbert Kritzer
University of Minnesota
Minneapolis, USA

Linda Mulcahy
Centre for Socio-Legal Studies
University of Oxford
Oxford, UK

Rosemary Hunter
University of Loughborough
Loughborough, UK

Carl Stychin
Institute of Advanced Legal Studies
University of London
London, UK

Mariana Valverde
Centre for Criminology & Socio-Legal Studies
University of Toronto
Toronto, Canada

Sally Wheeler
College of Law
Australian National University
Canberra, Australia

Senthorun Raj
Manchester Metropolitan University
Manchester, UK

The Palgrave Socio-Legal Studies series is a developing series of monographs and textbooks featuring cutting edge work which, in the best tradition of socio-legal studies, reach out to a wide international audience.

Paula Campos Pinto
Teresa Janela Pinto
Patrícia Neca • Fernando Fontes
Editors

Equal Rights, Equal Voices

The CRPD and the Pursuit of Legal Capacity for Persons with Intellectual and Psychosocial Disability

palgrave
macmillan

Editors
Paula Campos Pinto
Observatory on Disability and Human Rights and Interdisciplinary Centre on Gender Studies, Institute of Social and Political Sciences
University of Lisbon
Lisbon, Portugal

Teresa Janela Pinto
Observatory on Disability and Human Rights and Interdisciplinary Centre on Gender Studies, Institute of Social and Political Sciences
University of Lisbon
Lisbon, Portugal

Patrícia Neca
Observatory on Disability and Human Rights and Interdisciplinary Centre on Gender Studies, Institute of Social and Political Sciences
University of Lisbon
Lisbon, Portugal

Fernando Fontes
Centro de Estudos Sociais
University of Coimbra
Coimbra, Portugal

ISSN 2947-9274 ISSN 2947-9282 (electronic)
Palgrave Socio-Legal Studies
ISBN 978-3-032-05968-0 ISBN 978-3-032-05969-7 (eBook)
https://doi.org/10.1007/978-3-032-05969-7

This publication was funded by national funds through the Fundação para a Ciência e a Tecnologia, within the multiannual funding of the Interdisciplinary Center for Gender Studies (CIEG/ISCSP-ULisboa) - UIDP/04304/2020.

© The Editor(s) (if applicable) and The Author(s) 2026. This book is an open access publication.

Open Access This book is licensed under the terms of the Creative Commons Attribution 4.0 International License (http://creativecommons.org/licenses/by/4.0/), which permits use, sharing, adaptation, distribution and reproduction in any medium or format, as long as you give appropriate credit to the original author(s) and the source, provide a link to the Creative Commons license and indicate if changes were made.
The images or other third party material in this book are included in the book's Creative Commons license, unless indicated otherwise in a credit line to the material. If material is not included in the book's Creative Commons license and your intended use is not permitted by statutory regulation or exceeds the permitted use, you will need to obtain permission directly from the copyright holder.
The use of general descriptive names, registered names, trademarks, service marks, etc. in this publication does not imply, even in the absence of a specific statement, that such names are exempt from the relevant protective laws and regulations and therefore free for general use.
The publisher, the authors and the editors are safe to assume that the advice and information in this book are believed to be true and accurate at the date of publication. Neither the publisher nor the authors or the editors give a warranty, expressed or implied, with respect to the material contained herein or for any errors or omissions that may have been made. The publisher remains neutral with regard to jurisdictional claims in published maps and institutional affiliations.

This Palgrave Macmillan imprint is published by the registered company Springer Nature Switzerland AG.
The registered company address is: Gewerbestrasse 11, 6330 Cham, Switzerland

If disposing of this product, please recycle the paper.

Acknowledgments

This book owes its existence to many people and institutions.

First, we want to thank the Foundation for Science and Technology in Portugal (FCT) for providing the grant that enabled the development of the EQUAL project (EXPL/SOC-ASO/1326/2021), whose outcomes form the basis of this publication.

Project EQUAL was a collective enterprise that involved academic and non-academic researchers and several partners who are key actors in the disability—the *National Federation of Social Solidarity Cooperatives* (FENACERCI), the *National Federation of Entities for the Rehabilitation of People with Mental Illness* (FNERDM), and the *Portuguese Federation for Intellectual Disability* (HUMANITAS)—and the judicial and human rights field—the *Office of the Prosecutor General* (PGR), the *Ombudsman*, and the *High Council for the Judiciary*—as well as *CES, Centro de Estudos Sociais of the University of Coimbra.* For the joint effort of this large team, and especially the invaluable contribution of the four persons with intellectual and psychosocial disabilities who participated as non-academic researchers—Aretha Ribeiro, Artur Tavares, Cristina Espiney and Maria Adelaide Cruz—we are deeply grateful.

We also want to acknowledge the support of the Interdisciplinary Centre of Gender Studies (CIEG) of the Institute of Social and Political Sciences, University of Lisbon, for providing resources and assistance throughout the study and for enabling the open-access publication of this book (through the FCT funding UIDP/04304/2020).

Special thanks are due to Clelia Petracca and Kishor Kannan Ramesh at Springer for their precious guidance during the publication process, and to Inês Robalo and Eilionóir Flynn for enriching this publication with their chapters.

Above all, we are deeply indebted to all our interviewees, for their time and insights, but most particularly to *Oscar, Samuel, Sophie, Mary, John and Peter,* for so generously sharing with us their life stories, struggles and hopes. This book is also our tribute to them.

Contents

Notes on Contributors

Eilionóir Flynn PhD in Law, is an Established Professor at the School of Law and Director of the Centre for Disability Law and Policy (CDLP) at the National University of Ireland Galway. Her research interests include legal capacity, disability advocacy, reproductive justice, and the intersectionality of disability, gender, and ageing.

Fernando Fontes PhD in Sociology and Social Policy (University of Leeds-UK) is a Research Associate at the *Centro de Estudos Sociais* of the University of Coimbra, Portugal. His research interests include disability politics and policies, violence and disablist hate crime, disabled people's movements, disabled people's intimate citizenship and research methodologies. He has published widely at the national and international levels on these topics and is a member of the Editorial Board of Disability and Society.

Patrícia Neca PhD in Psychology, is an Invited Assistant Professor at ISCSP, the Institute of Social and Political Sciences of the University of Lisbon, Vice-Coordinator of the Disability and Human Rights Observatory, and an Integrated Researcher at the Interdisciplinary Centre for Gender Studies (CIEG). Her research focuses on the reception of legal innovation aimed at promoting the rights of persons with disabilities, particularly in the areas of access to employment, access to justice, inclusive education, but also on social representations and stereotyping of disability.

Paula Campos Pinto PhD in Sociology, is an Associate Professor at ISCSP, the Institute of Social and Political Sciences of the University of Lisbon, where she is also a founder and coordinator of the Disability and Human Rights Observatory and Deputy Director of CIEG, the Interdisciplinary Centre for Gender Studies. She has been the Principal Investigator and researcher in several national and international projects related to disability, human rights and gender intersections with disability, and the author of many national and international publications on these topics (https://paulacampospinto.com/).

Teresa Janela Pinto PhD in Social Policy, is an Assistant Professor at ISCSP, University of Lisbon. She is the Vice-Coordinator of the Disability and Human Rights Observatory (ODDH) and an Integrated Researcher at CIEG, the Interdisciplinary Centre for Gender Studies. She serves on the Ethics and Scientific Committee of the International Foundation of Applied Disability Research (FIRAH). Her research focuses on the governance and reform of social policies and social services, with particular attention to the challenges of advancing a rights-based approach in the fields of disability and gender. https://orcid.org/.

Inês Robalo is a Public Prosecutor, legal advisor to the Prosecutor General's Office, and member of the Central Authority for the Hague Convention on the International Protection of Adults.

Abbreviations

CACI	Centre of Activities and Capacitation for Inclusion
CAO	Occupational Activities Centre
CES	Centro de Estudos Sociais
CIEG	Interdisciplinary Centre for Gender Studies
CRPD	Convention on the Rights of Persons with Disabilities
EQUAL	Equality before the law and the right to self-determination of persons with intellectual and psychosocial disabilities in Portugal
FCT	Foundation for Science and Technology
FENACERCI	National Federation of Social Solidarity Cooperatives
FNERDM	National Federation of Entities for the Rehabilitation of People with Mental Illness
HUMANITAS	Portuguese Federation for Intellectual Disability
PGR	Prosecutor General's Office
UN	United Nations

List of Figures

1

Introduction: Rethinking Legal Capacity and Citizenship—Contributions from the Sociology of Human Rights

Paula Campos Pinto, Teresa Janela Pinto, Patrícia Neca, and Fernando Fontes

Abstract This chapter introduces the EQUAL project, which examined the legal capacity and self-determination of people with intellectual and psychosocial disabilities in Portugal. It critiques the historical linkage of citizenship to mental capacity and highlights the UN CRPD's Article 12, which calls for equal legal recognition for all and supported decision-making. Despite reforms like Portugal's Law 49/2018, practical barriers persist: medicalized capacity tests, substituted decision-making, and attitudinal, institutional, and structural barriers. The EQUAL study adopted

P. Campos Pinto (✉) • T. J. Pinto • P. Neca
Observatory on Disability and Human Rights and Interdisciplinary Centre on Gender Studies, Institute of Social and Political Sciences, University of Lisbon, Lisbon, Portugal
e-mail: mppinto@edu.ulisboa.pt; teresajpinto@iscsp.ulisboa.pt; pneca@iscsp.ulisboa.pt

F. Fontes
Centro de Estudos Sociais, University of Coimbra, Coimbra, Portugal
e-mail: fernandofontes@ces.uc.pt

© The Author(s) 2026

P. Campos Pinto et al. (eds.), *Equal Rights, Equal Voices*, Palgrave Socio-Legal Studies, https://doi.org/10.1007/978-3-032-05969-7_1

an interdisciplinary framework, drawing on theoretical insights from both sociological and legal scholarship. Methodologically, it combined court decisions analysis, interviews, focus groups, and six life stories using participatory methods to center disabled people's voices. The plan of the book is described.

Keywords Legal capacity • UNCRPD (article 12) • Self-determination • Sociology of human rights

The right to self-determination, defined as the ability to make decisions about one's own life and to participate in political decision-making, is seen as a key element of the modern ideal of citizenship (Kymlicka & Donaldson, 2017). In the past, some groups of people, such as women and racialised people, were considered incapable and unworthy of equal participation in the polity. However, current discourses on citizenship, at least in democratic regimes, assume its universal nature. Nevertheless, many members of society are still relegated, both *de facto* and *de jure*, to the status of passive subjects rather than active citizens. Indeed, prevailing notions, derived from the so-called *capacity contract* (Clifford, 2014; Simplican, 2015), tend to premise citizenship on mental capacity. Therefore, many persons with intellectual and/or psychosocial disabilities find themselves deprived of this right and are relegated to a status of permanent vulnerability, dependency and *civil death* (Quinn, 2021). This contributes to reinforcing their structural marginalisation in contemporary societies, ascribing them a status of *de-citizens* (Devlin & Pothier, 2005).

This traditional view has been challenged by the adoption, in 2006, of the UN Convention on the Rights of Persons with Disabilities (CRPD; United Nations, 2006). Article 12 of the CRPD is focused on legal capacity and marks the beginning of a new social, legal and political paradigm that recognises all people, regardless of the complexity of their needs, the right to "equality before the law, on equal terms with all other citizens, in all areas of their life". It also calls upon

States to eliminate barriers to full citizenship by providing "the support they may require in exercising their legal capacity".

Almost two decades after such a proclamation, these provisions are yet to be fully accomplished. Around the world, laws continue to confuse legal capacity with mental capacity and test for capacity through medical assessment (Keene et al., 2019). This also occurs in countries where legal reform has been undertaken, as in Portugal.

Uncovering these barriers and resistances and producing evidence to inform new laws, policies and practices that advance the human rights of all persons with disabilities have thus become critical research aims. This book presents findings from EQUAL,[1] *Equality before the law and the right to self-determination of persons with intellectual and psychosocial disabilities in Portugal*, a large and multi-actor study framed by inclusive research principles (Barnes, 2003). EQUAL set out to explore the challenges, barriers and opportunities surrounding the implementation of legal reform that sought to transpose to domestic law the standards of the CRPD regarding legal capacity and equality before the law. While drawing from a specific context—Portugal—the study aimed to contribute to a growing body of international work that critically examines laws that restrict or remove the exercise of human rights based on disability (e.g. Barton-Hanson, 2018; Keene et al., 2019; Martinez-Pujalte, 2019). However, unlike most of the existing literature that has addressed the topic of legal capacity (e.g. Donnelly et al., 2022; Flynn et al., 2019; Stein et al., 2021), this book is unique in bringing a sociological lens to the fore.

It centres on the stories and voices of people with intellectual and psychosocial disabilities whose legal capacity has been either withdrawn or significantly curtailed. These narratives, together with other data gathered through the EQUAL research, provide the basis on which we propose to explore the meaning of legal agency, participation, and citizenship for people with disabilities in contemporary societies, in order to understand their significance not only in legal and sociological theory but also in the lived realities of everyday life.

[1] For more information, please visit the website https://equal.iscsp.ulisboa.pt/

Theoretical Background

Our research was grounded in an interdisciplinary framework, drawing on theoretical insights from both sociological and legal scholarship. In human rights theory, legal capacity is described as a person's power or possibility to act within the framework of the legal system (de Bhailís & Flynn, 2017). It is what makes a human being a subject of law, able to make binding decisions, ranging from the most profound (choosing where and with whom to live or giving consent to a complex medical treatment) to everyday choices (e.g. to buy a bus ticket or to sign a lease).

Equality before the law, that is, legal capacity, is protected under international law (e.g. the Universal Declaration of Human Rights and the International Covenant on Civil and Political Rights), but of particular interest to us, in this book, is Article 12 of the CRPD, which is considered one of the most complex and challenging articles in this Convention (Arstein-Kerslake, 2016). According to the CRPD Committee, in its General Comment no. 1 (2014), legal capacity must be available to everyone without exception and involves both the capacity to be a rights' holder (*legal standing*), as well as the capacity to act under the law and engage in legal transactions and relationships (*legal agency*). Article 12 further calls on States to implement measures that ensure access to support in the exercise of legal capacity, as well as safeguards to protect from abuse and undue influence. These safeguards must, however, "respect the rights, will and preferences of the person, including the right to take risks and make mistakes" (UN Committee on the Rights of Persons with Disabilities, 2014, para.22).

This prescriptive nature of the CRPD (Lawson & Beckett, 2021) rendered visible the unsuitability and disrespect of long-established legal regulations towards the dignity and human rights of persons with disabilities. Following the ratification of the Convention, many countries undertook legal reforms to transpose into domestic law the standards of the CRPD. In Portugal, this included the publication of Law 49 of 14 August 2018, which introduced the new Accompanied Adult Regime. This law replaced the more rigid and paternalistic institute of *interdiction* (guardianship or substituted decision-making) with a more nuanced approach (Cordeiro, 2018). While previous legislation was based on the idea that persons with specific impairments (those with cognitive impairments, deaf and blind people, as well as those with mental illness and/or who abused of psychotropic substances) lacked the capacity to manage their lives and assets and therefore needed to be declared legally interdicted or incapacitated, the new regime, at least in theory, introduced the principle of *protection without incapacitation* (Monteiro, 2019), i.e. without removing a person's capacity to exercise their will and rights. Under the new law, it is up to the court to determine the level of support each individual requires and to define the appropriate support measures to be deployed.

If, in legal terms, capacity is what makes a person a subject of law, in sociological terms, it involves what it means to be human, because the life choices we make are part of who we are (Chapman et al., 2024; Quinn, 2010). As such, it is an important construct to analyse from a sociological perspective. Deprivation of legal capacity is also sociologically relevant because it affects a large group of people. Without the ability to make decisions, people with disabilities learn helplessness and dependence and are more likely to experience stereotyping, objectification and other forms of exclusion, which, in turn, contribute to their vulnerability and increase their risk of abuse and neglect (Arstein-Kerslake, 2016).

The emerging field of sociology of human rights (Pinto, 2023) analyses "the economic, political, social and cultural forces that impact the construction, interpretation, implementation, and enforcement of human rights norms, policies and laws" (Frezzo, 2015, pp. 1–2). Hence, it provides the concepts and theoretical frameworks to understand the extent to which legal tools, such as Law 49/2018 in Portugal, contribute to challenging the *capacity contract*, not just *de jure* but *de facto*, and the underlying political, social, and cultural forces that foster or hinder change.

Researchers developing an approach grounded on the sociology of human rights have noted how medical discourses and classifications, by labelling people with disabilities as incapable of rational thought and self-mastery, have provided the ground to restrain their rights and legitimise continuous supervision, coercive treatment, and paternalism in care (Rioux & Valentine, 2006). They have explored how particular social contexts and power relations, institutional arrangements, societal reactions and representations, and social control hinder the realisation of human rights (Pinto, 2018; Rioux & Valentine, 2006) and are often used to justify measures intended to "protect" persons with disabilities, even though it remains unclear whether persons under substituted decision-making legal regimes are safer, as they have fewer rights and are less than full citizens (Glen, 2015).

Likewise, in this book, by untangling disability-based relations of domination, we hope to contribute to expose the social processes through which dependency and vulnerability are produced and offer insights to help address the structural, institutional, and attitudinal barriers identified.

Methodological Approach

This study was carried out within the scope of the EQUAL Project, which brought together key institutional and civil society actors to explore the dynamics, challenges, and opportunities in the implementation of legal reform around legal capacity.[2] The project focused on persons with intellectual and psychosocial disabilities, as they are amongst the groups most commonly subject to legal restrictions on capacity through substituted decision-making regimes and continue to face barriers to equal recognition before the law (Webb et al., 2020). Thus, EQUAL examined how both formal and informal restrictions on the right to make decisions impact the agency, citizenship, and social participation of these two groups of persons with disabilities.

The study involved the examination of 747 legal judgments issued under the new law in three judicial districts (*comarcas*) of the country,

[2] Project promoted by the School of Social and Political Sciences (ISCSP–ULisboa), in partnership with the three largest federations of organisations in the field of intellectual and psychosocial disability in Portugal: the National Federation of Social Solidarity Cooperatives (FENACERCI), the National Federation of Entities for the Rehabilitation of People with Mental Illness (FNERDM), and the Portuguese Federation for Intellectual Disability (HUMANITAS). The project consortium also included key legal institutions responsible for implementing legal capacity legislation and safeguarding individual rights: the Prosecutor General's Office (PGR), the Ombudsman, and the High Council for the Judiciary.

representing urban, rural and semi-urban contexts, in order to identify patterns in court decisions. It also included 31 interviews with key stakeholders (judges, prosecutors, experts responsible for medico-legal and social assessments, directors and staff from disability service providers, and family members of persons with intellectual or psychosocial disabilities).

To bring forward the voice of persons with psychosocial and intellectual disabilities and obtain a better understanding of their rights' experiences, especially the barriers and challenges they face to achieve self-determination in everyday life, we conducted four focus groups with 19 participants. We also undertook an in-depth analysis of six case studies focusing on four men and two women with intellectual or psychosocial disabilities who had experienced restrictions on their legal capacity. Their life stories and, whenever possible, the discourse analysis of their rulings and other processual documents enabled the development of sociological portraits (Lahire, 2002) that furthered our understanding of the formal and informal barriers to social participation and full citizenship.

Methodologically, this study adopted a participatory approach guided by human rights principles, promoting the active involvement of persons with disabilities and their organisations in all stages of the research (Pinto et al., 2024). Four non-academic researchers who identify as persons with intellectual or psychosocial disabilities contributed to the data analysis and played a particularly active role in preparing, conducting, and analysing the findings from the focus groups. A variety of visual tools—some developed specifically for this project—were used in these sessions. Drawing on their lived experiences, these researchers provided rich insights that were key to illuminate our discussions and deepen our understanding of the issues at stake.

Plan of the Book

Our book differs from other studies that have addressed the right to legal capacity by focusing on a discussion of legal concepts and regimes (e.g. Donnelly et al., 2022; Stein et al., 2021). Instead, this book brings forward the voice of persons with disabilities through the examination of the life stories of six persons with intellectual and psychosocial disability, which form the backbone of our discussions. Thus, the book is organised into two parts.

Part I sets the stage by providing an understanding of legal capacity regimes and offering a panoramic view of the main findings of the EQUAL project. In Chap. 2, Eilionóir Flynn examines the human rights norms established in Article 12 of the CRPD on the right to legal capacity. Assessing how different domestic legal systems have replaced adult guardianship and substituted decision-making regimes with supported decision-making systems that recognise disabled people's autonomy and respect their will and preferences, she draws lessons for legal reform efforts across the globe. Pursuing this analysis, the following chapter, by Inês Robalo, assesses, from a legal perspective, the foundation, key features, strengths and limitations of the legal capacity reform in Portugal, enacted by Law 49 of 14 August 2018. Finally, Chap. 4 presents the key findings of the EQUAL project, drawing from the analyses of court decisions, interviews with stakeholders and focus groups with persons with disabilities.

Part II presents the six life stories. Through the voices of Oscar, Samuel, Mary, Sophie, John and Peter we learn about the kinds of barriers that persons with intellectual and psychosocial disabilities continue to face to exercise their legal capacity, and about their struggles for inclusion and self-determination.

Finally, the concluding chapter brings together all the data, presenting a cross-case synthesis that identifies the similarities and differences between the six case studies analysed, integrating them with data from the other strands of the study. It argues that achieving equality before the law and legal agency for persons with intellectual and psychosocial disabilities requires more than just legal reform. It involves a paradigm shift in social representations and attitudes towards disability, as well as progress in all areas of rights, as human rights are indivisible, interdependent, and interconnected. We also offer insights for law, policy and practice reform that improve equality, self-determination and full citizenship for all persons with disabilities in contemporary societies.

A final word on the terminology. Throughout this book, we primarily use the term *persons with disabilities* and its variants, in alignment with the language of the UN CRPD. We also use the term *disabled people* in acknowledgement of a sociopolitical understanding of disability as a form of social oppression. When referring to the new legal capacity law in Portugal, we occasionally adopt the expression *Accompanied Adult Regime*, along with related terms such as *accompanied adult*, *accompanied person*, and *accompanying person*, as these terms reflect the official terminology of the new law. However, for reasons of clarity, flow, and alignment with the vocabulary more frequently used in the Anglo-Saxon legal capacity literature, we often also interchange these terms with *supported person* and *support person* or *supporter*.

References

Arstein-Kerslake, A. (2016). An Empowering Dependency: Exploring Support for the Exercise of Legal Capacity. *Scandinavian Journal of Disability Research, 18*(1), 77–92. https://doi.org/10.1080/15017419.2014.941926

Barnes, C. (2003). What a Difference a Decade Makes: Reflections on Doing 'Emancipatory Disability Research'. *Disability & Society, 18*(1), 3–17.

Barton-Hanson, R. (2018). Reforming Best Interests: The Road Towards Supported Decision-Making. *Journal of Social Welfare and Family Law, 40*(3), 277–298. https://doi.org/10.1080/09649069.2018.1493650

Chapman, K., Dixon, A., Ehrlich, C., & Kendall, E. (2024). Dignity and the Importance of Acknowledgement of Personhood for People with Disability. *Qualitative Health Research, 34*(1–2), 141–153. https://doi.org/10.1177/10497323231204562

Clifford, S. (2014). Politics, Groups, and Identities the Capacity Contract: Locke, Disability, and the Political Exclusion of "Idiots". *Politics, Groups, and Identities, 2*, 90–103. https://doi.org/10.1080/21565503.2013.876918

Cordeiro, A. M. (2018). Da situação jurídica do maior acompanhado. Estudo de política legislativa relativo a um novo regime das denominadas incapacidades dos maiores. *Revista de Direito Civil, Ano III, 2018*, 473–554.

de Bhailís, C., & Flynn, E. (2017). Recognising Legal Capacity: Commentary and Analysis of Article 12 CRPD. *International Journal of Law in Context, 13*(1), 6–21. https://doi.org/10.1017/S174455231600046X

Devlin, R., & Pothier, D. (2005). Introduction: Toward a Critical Theory of Dis-Citizenship. In *Critical Disability Theory…Essays in Philosophy, Politics, Policy, and Law* (pp. 1–22). University of British Columbia Press.
Donnelly, M., Harding, R., & Taşcioğlu, E. (2022). *Supporting Legal Capacity in Socio-Legal Context*. Hart Publishing.
Flynn, E., Arstein-Kerslake, A., De Bhailís, C., & Serra, M. L. (2019). *Global Perspectives on Legal Capacity Reform: Our Voices, Our Stories*. Routledge.
Frezzo, M. (2015). *The Sociology of Human Rights*. Polity Press.
Glen, K. B. (2015). Supported Decision-Making and the Human Right of Legal Capacity. *INCLUSION, 3*(1), 2–16. https://doi.org/10.1352/2326-6988-3.1.2
Keene, A. R., Kane, N. B., Kim, S. Y. H., & Owen, G. S. (2019). Taking Capacity Seriously? Ten Years of Mental Capacity Disputes Before England's Court of Protection. *International Journal of Law and Psychiatry, 62*(January–February), 56–76. https://doi.org/10.1016/J.IJLP.2018.11.005
Kymlicka, W., & Donaldson, S. (2017). Inclusive Citizenship Beyond the Capacity Contract. In A. Shachar, R. Buabock, I. Bloemraad, & M. Vink (Eds.), *The Oxford Handbook of Citizenship* (pp. 838–860). Oxford University Press.
Lahire, B. (2002). *Portraits sociologiques: Dispositions et variations individuelles*. Nathan.
Lawson, A., & Beckett, A. E. (2021). The Social and Human Rights Models of Disability: Towards a Complementarity Thesis. *The International Journal of Human Rights, 25*(2), 348–379.
Martinez-Pujalte, A. (2019). Legal Capacity and Supported Decision-Making: Lessons from Some Recent Legal Reforms. *Laws, 8*(1), 4. https://doi.org/10.3390/LAWS8010004
Monteiro, A. (2019). Das incapacidades ao maior acompanhado. Breve apresentação da Lei nº 49/2018. *Revista de Legislação e de Jurisprudência, 4013*, 87–107.
Pinto, P. C. (2018). Por uma sociologia pública: repensar a deficiência na ótica dos direitos humanos. *Análise Social, 53*(229), 1010–1035. https://doi.org/10.31447/AS00032573.2018229.07
Pinto, P. C. (2023). Disability and Human Rights. In R. L. Brown, M. Maroto, & D. Pettinicchio (Eds.), *The Oxford Handbook of the Sociology of Human Rights* (pp. 175–194). Oxford University Press.
Pinto, P. C., Pinto, T. J., Neca, P., & Maltez, B. (2024). Doing Inclusive Research Guided by Human Rights Principles with Persons with Intellectual and Psychosocial Disabilities: Potential and Challenges. *Sage Research Methods: Diversifying and Decolonizing Research*. https://doi.org/10.4135/9781529691160

Quinn, G. (2010). Personhood & Legal Capacity: Perspectives on the Paradigm Shift of Article 12. *Paper Presented at the HPOD Conference, February 2010.*

Quinn, G. (2021). Reconsidering Personhood—From 'Civil Death' to 'Civil Life' for Persons with Disabilities: Reflections on Article 12 of the UN Convention on the Rights of Persons with Disabilities. In B. Nehal, F. Hoffmann, F. Mégret, & M. Satterthwaite (Eds.), *The Struggle for Human Rights* (pp. 160–173). Oxford University Press.

Rioux, M. H., & Valentine, F. (2006). Does Theory Matter? Exploring the Nexus between Disability, Human Rights and Public Policy. In D. Pothier & R. Devlin (Eds.), *Critical Disability Theory: Essays in Philosophy, Politics, Policy and Law* (pp. 47–69). UBC Press.

Simplican, S. C. (2015). *The Capacity Contract: Intellectual Disability and the Question of Citizenship*. University of Minnesota Press.

Stein, M. A., Mahomed, F., Patel, V., & Sunkel, C. (2021). *Mental Health, Legal Capacity, and Human Rights*. In *Mental Health, Legal Capacity, and Human Rights*. Cambridge University Press.

UN Committee on the Rights of Persons with Disabilities. (2014). *General Comment No. 1: Article 12 – Equal Recognition Before the Law.*

United Nations. (2006). *Convention on the Rights of Persons with Disabilities (A/RES/61/106).* https://www.un.org/disabilities/documents/convention/convoptprot-e.pdf

Webb, P., Davidson, G., Edge, R., Falls, D., Keenan, F., Kelly, B., McLaughlin, A., Montgomery, L., Mulvenna, C., Norris, B., Owens, A., & Shea Irvine, R. (2020). Key Components of Supporting and Assessing Decision Making Ability. *International Journal of Law and Psychiatry, 72.* https://doi.org/10.1016/j.ijlp.2020.101613

Open Access This chapter is licensed under the terms of the Creative Commons Attribution 4.0 International License (http://creativecommons.org/licenses/by/4.0/), which permits use, sharing, adaptation, distribution and reproduction in any medium or format, as long as you give appropriate credit to the original author(s) and the source, provide a link to the Creative Commons license and indicate if changes were made.

The images or other third party material in this chapter are included in the chapter's Creative Commons license, unless indicated otherwise in a credit line to the material. If material is not included in the chapter's Creative Commons license and your intended use is not permitted by statutory regulation or exceeds the permitted use, you will need to obtain permission directly from the copyright holder.

Part I

Setting the Scene: CRPD and Legal Capacity Reform

2

Legal Capacity in Global Perspective: Translating International Human Rights Norms in Domestic Legal Systems

Eilionóir Flynn

Abstract This chapter will examine the human rights norms established in Article 12 of the CRPD regarding the right to legal capacity. It will explore how pushback against these norms has emerged and how this interacts with states' efforts to work towards full compliance with Article 12. This chapter will assess how different domestic legal systems have achieved the repeal of adult guardianship and substituted decision-making regimes and replaced these with supported decision-making systems that recognise disabled people's autonomy and respect their will and preferences. In so doing, it will consider what lessons can be learned from legal systems where reforms on Article 12 have occurred to date for others engaged in similar reform efforts across the globe.

Keywords Legal capacity • Law reform • Global perspectives • Article 12 CRPD

E. Flynn (✉)
Centre for Disability Law and Policy, School of Law, University of Galway, Galway, Ireland
e-mail: eilionoir.flynn@nuigalway.ie

© The Author(s) 2026

P. Campos Pinto et al. (eds.), *Equal Rights, Equal Voices*, Palgrave Socio-Legal Studies,
https://doi.org/10.1007/978-3-032-05969-7_2

Introduction

Since the entry into force of the United Nations Convention on the Rights of Persons with Disabilities (CRPD) in 2008, the right to equal recognition before the law enshrined in Article 12 has been one of the aspects of the CRPD that States have most struggled to implement in full. Recognising the difficulties States faced in interpreting this right in practice, the United Nations Committee on the Rights of Persons (the Committee) chose to adopt its first ever General Comment on this subject in 2014. Following the adoption of General Comment 1, several countries have initiated legislative reforms related to legal capacity which recognise forms of supported decision-making. All these countries have referred to the CRPD and to Article 12, in particular, as one of the driving forces of these reforms, but in many cases, their compliance with the requirements of General Comment 1 leaves much to be desired (Flynn, 2021; Marshall et al., 2023; Constantino Caycho & Bregaglio Lazarte, 2023). At the same time, pushback has escalated against the Committee and its position on Article 12, as articulated in General Comment 1, among scholars and States alike, who are critical of the Committee's radical approach to autonomy, which they see as being taken too far (Freeman et al., 2015; Szmukler 2019, Ruck Keene et al., 2023).

This chapter will examine the human rights norms established in Article 12 of the CRPD, as interpreted in General Comment 1. It will explore how pushback against these norms has emerged, and how this interacts with States' efforts to work towards full compliance with Article 12. Based on the Committee's interpretation of Article 12, this chapter will assess how different domestic legal systems have achieved the repeal of adult guardianship and substituted decision-making regimes and replaced these with supported decision-making systems that recognise disabled people's autonomy and respect their will and preferences. In so doing, it will consider what lessons can be learned from legal systems where reforms on Article 12 have occurred to date for others engaged in similar reform efforts across the globe.

Requirements of Article 12 and General Comment 1

Article 12, at its core, requires states to recognise that 'persons with disabilities enjoy legal capacity on an equal basis with others in all aspects of life.' This presents a significant challenge to states engaging in legal capacity law reform, as it requires a review of many different areas of law. These include, but are not limited to, the law of contract, laws governing marriage and divorce, property and inheritance laws, consent to medical treatment, consent to sex, and many other areas. The main areas in which states have concentrated their law reform efforts on Article 12 to date are in the realm of adult guardianship laws, or in the words of the Committee, laws relating to 'substituted decision-making.' Since its first Concluding Observations on this topic, the Committee has been urging states to 'take action to develop laws and policies to replace regimes of substitute decision-making by supported decision-making' (Committee on the Rights of Persons with Disabilities, 2010, 2011).

Prior to the adoption of General Comment 1, some sceptics argued that because the text of Article 12 did not specify the requirement to abolish all forms of substituted decision-making, the Committee had exceeded its authority by requiring States to achieve this standard in its Concluding Observations (Freeman et al., 2015). Similarly, they argued that Article 12(4), which refers to 'safeguards' in measures 'relating to the exercise of legal capacity,' should be interpreted to allow for the continued existence of substituted decision-making regimes such as adult guardianship (Szmukler et al., 2014). However, the Committee has remained consistent in its interpretation that Article 12 does require the abolition of all forms of substituted decision-making and has now provided a definition of substituted decision-making in General Comment 1 (Committee on the Rights of Persons with Disabilities, 2014). This definition clarifies that a substitute decision-making regime is one in which:

(i) legal capacity is removed from a person, even if this is in respect of a single decision;

(ii) a substitute decision-maker can be appointed by someone other than the person concerned, and this can be done against his or her will; or

(iii) any decision made by a substitute decision-maker is based on what is believed to be in the objective 'best interests' of the person concerned, as opposed to being based on the person's own will and preferences (para. 27, 2014).

In the initially published version of the General Comment, the clause between sections (ii) and (iii) used the term 'and' instead of 'or.' This typographical error was corrected in a subsequent document published by the Committee (2018). This distinction is important because it clarifies that all three criteria do not need to be present in a legal system before it can be described as a substituted decision-making regime. Instead, the presence of any one of these three characteristics is sufficient to meet the definition of substituted decision-making.

The General Comment also clarifies what should be considered disability discrimination in the denial of legal capacity. By drawing on the CRPD's prohibition of disability discrimination 'in purpose or effect,' it demonstrates that even where adult guardianship laws in practice disproportionately result in disabled people being denied legal capacity, they run contrary to the requirements of Article 12 (para. 25, 2014). This is so even where the relevant domestic laws do not include explicit criteria regarding the individual's disability or impairment, but rely on general concepts of mental incapacity, or lack of insight, or ability to appreciate the consequences of decisions. In this way, the General Comment distinguishes between the concepts of 'mental capacity' and 'legal capacity' and requires states to cease using determinations of an individual's 'mental capacity' or decision-making ability to restrict or deny that person's exercise of legal capacity (para. 14, 2014). Importantly, it clarifies that assessments of an individual's mental capacity, whether based on status, outcome or functional approaches, should not be used to determine whether an individual is recognised as a person who can exercise their legal capacity (para. 15, 2014).

The General Comment provides a broad conceptualisation of what support for exercising legal capacity can look like in different legal systems (para. 29(a)–(i), 2014). The core criteria it outlines can be broadly categorised into three general areas: making supports available to all, ensuring the centrality of will and preferences, and providing legal recognition for support. In the first category, the General Comment requires States to ensure that individuals' methods of communication are not a barrier to accessing support (para. 29(c), 2014). This is especially important when the person's methods of communication are not easily understood by others and can only be accurately interpreted by a few people who know them well. Similarly, the General Comment specifies that the person's level of support need should not be a barrier to accessing support to exercise legal capacity (para. 29(a), 2014). This is particularly the case for people with a high level of support need.

In making this requirement clear, the Committee is ensuring that States do not feel they have met the requirements of Article 12 by introducing forms of supported decision-making that only work well for people with low support needs who can clearly communicate their will and preferences in ways that are easily understood by others. Furthermore, the General Comment specifies that the person's financial means should not present barriers to accessing support to exercise legal capacity and that States must ensure that supports are available at nominal or no cost to the individual disabled person (para 29(e), 2014). Finally, the General Comment requires that new non-discriminatory methods are used to determine the person's support needs (para. 29(i), 2014). This means that functional assessments of mental capacity cannot be used to determine an individual's eligibility for support to exercise their legal capacity.

The second set of criteria for measures to support the exercise of legal capacity specified in the General Comment relates to the centrality of respect for the will and preferences of the person. This includes ensuring that individuals must be free to refuse the offer of support to exercise legal capacity and must be able to terminate support arrangements they have created at any time they choose (para. 29(g), 2014). Similarly, the General Comment clarifies that the fact that an individual uses support to exercise legal capacity in one aspect of their lives should not be used to justify any restrictions or denials of their legal capacity in other areas (para. 29(f), 2014). For example, if a person uses support to exercise their legal capacity in respect of financial decisions, this fact should not be used to justify restricting their rights to marry and found a family. The General Comment re-emphasises that all safeguards used in relation to exercises of legal capacity must be grounded in respect for the will and preferences of the person (para. 29(b), 2014). This means that the use of paternalistic criteria such as best interests is not permitted as a safeguard in supported decision-making regimes.

The third and final element of systems to support the exercise of legal capacity addressed in the General Comment is the need for States to legally recognise different forms of support arrangements related to the exercise of legal capacity. This must include mechanisms for third parties to verify the identity of a support person, as well as a mechanism for third parties to challenge the action of a support person if they believe they are not acting in accordance with the will and preferences of the person concerned (para. 29(d)–(h), 2014). Finally, the Committee clarifies that in order to provide legal recognition of these supports, States have an obligation to facilitate the creation of support, particularly for people who are isolated and may not have access to naturally occurring support in the community (para, 29(e), 2014).

The Committee's conceptualisation of support in the General Comment is open-ended, recognising that our knowledge and experience of support to exercise legal capacity is constantly evolving. This approach also acknowledges that different legal, social, economic, and cultural contexts may use different ways to recognise support to exercise legal capacity. Further, it requires that all legislative reforms adopted to meet this goal must be achieved with the meaningful and effective participation of persons with disabilities and their representative organisations (para. 50(c), 2014).

Importantly, the Committee took a deliberate decision not to enumerate specific examples of good practice from particular States, despite intense pressure, especially from States Parties, to do so (Arstein-Kerslake & Flynn, 2016). This was deliberate because the Committee understood that at the point when the General Comment was adopted in 2014, there were no examples globally of laws which fully complied with its requirements. The Committee did not want to praise in a General Comment laws which recognised certain forms of supported decision-making which existed in jurisdictions that still maintained substituted decision-making regimes (e.g. British Columbia and Sweden). It was further cognisant of how laws on paper may appear to be in compliance with the requirements set out in the General Comment, but in practice, their implementation may continue to perpetuate discrimination against disabled people, especially those with more complex support needs. Without the opportunity to fully explore the implementation of such laws with the representative organisations of persons with disabilities in all of the relevant jurisdictions, the Committee chose not to name specific laws as examples for States to follow in the General Comment.

One of the common critiques of the General Comment was that it did not adequately address the issue of the so-called 'hard cases' which challenge the general principle of respecting the individual's will and preferences in any decisions with legal consequences which must be made (Freeman et al., 2015). While the Committee did not enumerate all the possible hard cases which arise under Article 12, I have previously argued (Arstein-Kerslake & Flynn, 2016) that it does provide sufficient guidance for dealing with challenging situations that can be used to address the so-called hard cases.

I will consider three types of 'hard case' here in respect of support to exercise legal capacity. The first is where a person's will and preferences regarding a decision are impossible to identify, even after concerted efforts have been made to discover them. This would include, for example, a person in a coma who has left no specific instructions about whether or not they wish to be maintained on life support. In this case, the General Comment acknowledges that a person may be designated by law to make a decision based on the 'best interpretation' possible of that individual's will and preferences (para, 21, 2014), using all information they can access about that person's values and previous life choices, including information gathered from those who know the person well and can provide insight into the person's will and preferences.

The second 'hard case' is where the person's will and preferences are clearly communicated, but if followed, would result in serious harm to the person or others. While the General Comment does not explicitly address this scenario, it provides important principles which can be drawn upon in responding to this situation. As I have previously argued (Arstein-Kerslake & Flynn, 2016), there is nothing in either the text of

Article 12 nor in the General Comment which demands support persons to respect the individual's will and preferences where doing so would implicate them in civil or criminal liability at the domestic level (para. 13, 2014).

Different legal systems have different systems for addressing these risks of harm. In some jurisdictions, only harm to others is legally prohibited through civil and criminal law, whereas in others, legal liability also applies to individuals engaging in self-harm (Flynn & Arstein-Kerslake, 2017). While the content of these laws is often highly problematic from a disability human rights perspective, a detailed consideration of these issues is beyond the scope of the present chapter. As a starting point in addressing these complex situations, however, it is important to recall that the equal recognition of legal capacity also means that persons with disabilities should have legal responsibility for their actions on an equal basis with non-disabled people, including in the criminal justice system. As long as these standards are applied in a non-discriminatory way to persons with disabilities, on an equal basis with persons without disabilities, there should be no conflict with Article 12.

The third and final hard case relates to where a person's will and preferences are in conflict with each other. This may occur, for example, where a person expresses a desire to be free of pain but refuses to consent to a medical intervention which could alleviate that pain (Arstein-Kerslake & Flynn, 2016). Another common example is a person experiencing anorexia who has a will to live but whose preference is not to eat, and they may also refuse nasogastric feeding. Again, this is a situation in which the 'best interpretation' principle established in the General Comment would also apply (para. 21, 2014), especially where the person has not created an advance healthcare directive which would specify how such conflicts can be resolved should they arise. The process of arriving at a 'best interpretation' that can effectively resolve the apparent conflict between the individual's overarching will and their immediate preferences is a complex one, requiring deep consideration of what the person wants to prioritise in that specific set of circumstances, based on all available knowledge and information regarding their will and preferences.

These so-called hard cases will always be complex and difficult to resolve, regardless of the paradigm within which they are addressed.

However, I contend that it is substantively different to address these challenges using respect for will and preference as the overarching principle, rather than paternalistic concepts of 'best interests.' Approaching complex challenges using the will and preference paradigm ensures that the process by which the outcome is achieved is rooted in human rights norms developed by and with persons with disabilities themselves.

Backlash Against the Position of the General Comment

Prior to the General Comment's adoption, States and commentators alike had consistently called on the Committee to provide clarity on the types of substituted decision-making prohibited by Article 12 and on the kinds of supported decision-making that should be developed to replace them. However, once the Committee provided this clarity, there was significant backlash against the position it established in the General Comment. Some commentators have described its content as impractical and radical (University of Cambridge, Cambridge Intellectual & Developmental Disabilities Research Group, 2014). Others have claimed that the Committee's position is not 'legitimate' because it differs in some respects from the positions of other international human rights bodies, such as the European Court of Human Rights and the United Nations Human Rights Committee (Ruck Keene et al., 2023). As part of the challenge to the Committee's legitimacy, some commentators have pointed to the fact that not all persons with disabilities support the Committee's contention that legal capacity is a universal attribute and that everyone, no matter how significant their impairment, can express their will and preferences (Plumb, 2015).

At the root of much of the criticism from both scholars and State Parties is the underlying assumption that domestic legal frameworks must have a basis for intervention to prevent a person from taking decisions that would be dangerous to themselves or others. Similarly, critics contend that if States were truly to abolish the use of functional assessments of mental capacity to determine the exercise of legal capacity as defined in the General Comment, there would remain no human rights-compliant mechanism to assess the extent to which a person should be held accountable for their actions and should experience the consequences of those actions. However, supporters of the General Comment and the Committee's position do not agree that States will have no basis for intervention to protect individuals from harmful consequences if functional assessments of mental capacity and other regimes of substituted decision-making are removed (Flynn & Arstein-Kerslake, 2017). They simply argue that new, non-discriminatory, human rights-compliant mechanisms must be found that are not paternalistic in purpose or effect and that protect the totality of disabled people's human rights, rather than simply the person's right to be kept safe from harm (Flynn and Arstein-Kerslake, 2017).

The history and contemporary experiences of disabled people globally demonstrate that harmful practices, including segregation, institutionalisation, and forced treatment, were justified on the basis that they would keep people 'safe.' Disabled people's realities are that these practices often cause further harm and the violation of their human rights. Proponents of the General Comment, including this author, contend that the best way to keep people safe is not to protect them from any possible accountability or prevent them from making decisions that may be perceived by others as dangerous. It is to treat them on an equal basis with others by foregrounding respect for the person's will and preferences. This requires taking all possible measures to acknowledge, interpret, and act upon the person's will and preferences and ensure protection from liability for third parties who, in good faith, respect the person's will and preferences as expressed directly or interpreted by those who have chosen.

Despite the clarity provided by the Committee in General Comment 1, the backlash against this position continues to proliferate. This can be evidenced beyond the scholarship and commentary, for example, in subsequent State Reports to the Committee (Norway, 2015; Australia, 2019; Canada, 2022). Moreover, States like Ireland, which ratified the Convention after the adoption of the General Comment, continued to insert reservations on Article 12 (2018). The majority of countries which have ratified the Convention have made no efforts to reform their domestic laws on legal capacity. Among the countries which have engaged in domestic law reform on legal capacity following critique from the Committee in Concluding Observations or the adoption of the General Comment, the majority have not ensured full compliance with the requirements of Article 12 as interpreted in the General Comment (Bach & Espejo-Yaksic, 2023). This is true even among the countries which refer to Article 12 as one of the driving forces of their domestic law reform process, as will be discussed further in the following section. As a result, it is important to scrutinise some key elements of the reforms which have been completed since the entry into force of the CRPD and the adoption of the General Comment to understand the ways in which States are applying, and in some cases misapplying, these human rights standards in practice to domestic legal frameworks.

Application of Article 12 at National Level in Legal Capacity Law Reforms

It has been acknowledged by several commentators and by the Committee itself that no State is in perfect compliance with all of the obligations of the CRPD. This is particularly the case when it comes to the application of Article 12, especially given the broad scope of that Article which extends to 'all aspects of law' as discussed above. Nevertheless, it is worth examining some examples of the different ways in which States have sought to interpret their obligations under Article 12 and the General Comment in their reforms of adult guardianship laws and the introduction of supported decision-making regimes. Below, I will refer to examples of law reform in Austria, Colombia, Costa Rica, Ireland and Peru. A detailed exploration of each of the reforms in these countries is beyond the scope of this chapter; therefore, I draw only on aspects of those systems that relate to the criteria outlined in the General Comment, with respect to the shift in language and concepts, the conceptualisation of support, the provision of support and the legal recognition of support. The examples of law reforms in this section are by no means an exhaustive list of those which have occurred since the adoption of the General Comment. These specific examples have been chosen because, in each one, the State has drawn upon Article 12 in its justification for amending its existing law. All of the relevant States claim that these laws ensure compliance with Article 12, but the reality on the ground is far more complex. Nevertheless, each of these law reform processes contains important lessons which can be drawn on by grassroots movements and lawmakers in jurisdictions willing to embrace the challenge presented by Article 12.

In this section, I will explore four key dimensions of the relevant domestic reforms. The first relates to a shift in the language and concepts used to describe the exercise of legal capacity by persons with disabilities. This includes the introduction of the principle of will and preferences in the relevant domestic legal frameworks and the abolition of paternalistic concepts used to justify the imposition of substituted decision-making such as 'best interests' or 'incapacity to govern their decisions.' The second dimension relates to the different ways in which supports to exercise legal capacity are conceptualised in domestic law, ranging from a very prescriptive list of possible support arrangements to a more open-ended conceptualisation of support. The third dimension relates to the different ways in which support can be provided under the law, including support from family members and friends (naturally occurring supports) to the provision of independent supporters by the State. The fourth and final dimension relates to the different mechanisms by which support arrangements can be legally recognised, ranging from the authorisation of support arrangements by notaries public to formal approval by courts or tribunals of a particular support arrangement.

The Paradigm Shift in Language: Real or Superficial Change?

One of the most significant human rights victories in the development of new domestic legislation on Article 12 is the abolition of paternalistic concepts such as 'best interests' and their replacement with a guiding principle of respect for the will and preferences of the person. This has been achieved in the legislation of Ireland, Peru, and Colombia, for example. While reforms in these countries deliberately abolished the forms of adult guardianship which were previously imposed specifically on disabled people (respectively, wardship, guardianship, and judicial interdiction), some apparently disability-neutral limits on legal capacity remain which may in their application discriminate against persons with disabilities 'in purpose or effect.' For example, in Peru, restrictions on legal capacity remain in place for those experiencing addiction ('habitual drunkards' and 'drug addicts') and people who mismanaged their finances ('bad administrators' or 'prodigals') (Constantino Caycho, 2020). On their face, these are not disability-specific restrictions on legal capacity, but in practice, careful monitoring will be required to ensure that these options do not become default replacements for the system of adult guardianship previously imposed on persons with disabilities.

Another area of interest in these new legislative reforms is the terminology used to describe decision-makers of the last resort, who must interpret and act upon the will and preferences of the person concerned. Most jurisdictions have moved away from terms associated with adult guardianship systems in their legislative reforms. In others, terms similar to those previously used are maintained, including 'curator' in the Spanish law reform for the judicially appointed decision-maker (Ribot Igualada, 2023). In some cases, the conceptualisation uses a different term if the decision-maker can be appointed without the person's express consent. For example, decision-making representative is the term used in Ireland, which is distinct from the decision-making assistant or co-decision-maker, who can only be appointed by the person concerned. By contrast, in Peru, the judicial appointment of such a supporter without the express consent of the individual concerned is only possible when the person is in a coma, and therefore, the term used still relates to 'support' rather than 'representation' or 'administration' (Vasquez, 2021).

The reasoning for the different choices in terminology is not always clear. When new terminology is created for these roles, it can help signify a break with old paternalistic systems. However, we must not assume that a new label or term will inevitably lead to new approaches (Flynn, 2021). The underlying definitions and powers of these roles must be examined to assess the extent to which the system actually conforms to the guidance set out in the General Comment. No matter the term used to describe their role, if decision-makers can be appointed over the objections of the person concerned, if the person is not free to act independently should they wish to and must have their decisions validated by an appointed person before they will be legally recognised, and if individuals are not permitted to use their chosen form of support based on assessments of their mental capacity, these do not conform to the requirements of a support system established in the General Comment and still require further substantive reforms.

Different Ways of Conceptualising Support: From Open-Ended to Prescriptive

Law reforms at the domestic level have taken a wide range of approaches to the conceptualisation of support. Costa Rica, one of the first countries to reform its law following the adoption of the General Comment, did not precisely specify what constituted a 'support' measure within the legislative reform itself (Marshall et al., 2023). Its legislation authorises the designation of a legal person to provide support to exercise legal capacity, which implies that the supporter could be a natural person or a legally recognised organisation or entity. The precise powers of a supporter or the conditions under which they can be appointed and operate, were deliberately not prescribed by the initial Costa Rican legislation. This was done with the aim of involving civil society organisations, especially the representative organisations of persons with disabilities in a more participatory process to determine what support measures should be available, which would be provided for in subsequent regulations, rather than in the main text of the legislative reform (Constantino Caycho & Bregaglio Lazarte, 2023).

The advantage of this approach is that it recognises the need for flexibility and the time required to meaningfully engage with disabled people and their representative organisations, to arrive at a consensus on the types of support people actually want and how they should function at a practical level. However, taking such an open-ended approach to the conceptualisation of support also carries some risks. As with all law reforms on legal capacity, vigilance is required to ensure that the supports eventually designated by regulation are not so ambiguous as to be interpreted to enable substituted decision-making regimes to re-emerge simply rebranded as support measures.

The vast majority of legislative reforms have taken the opposite approach and precisely set out the different types of support to exercise legal capacity which will be recognised under new legal frameworks. Many of these reforms have taken decades to develop, and some have involved more participatory drafting processes than others. The precise mechanisms for support enshrined in these laws include advance planning mechanisms, such as enduring powers of attorney and advance healthcare directives. Most of the legislative reforms provide a mechanism for individuals to designate their chosen supporters, and some also provide a mechanism by which trusted supporters can have their role as interpreters of the person's will and preferences recognised. All jurisdictions which have engaged in these law reforms also provide a role for courts or tribunals to designate either a supporter or substitute decision-maker for a relevant person where they have not already appointed one and a decision with legal consequences needs to be made.

From this wide range of approaches, two key considerations emerge for those engaged in legal capacity reform. The first is the need for the specific types of support arrangement to be designed using grassroots-led approaches, informed by the lived experiences of disabled people and their supporters. This takes time in order to ensure meaningful participation, especially for those whose forms of communication are not easily understood by others. The second related consideration is that lawmakers are generally reluctant to abolish all forms of substituted decision-making without a clear roadmap of the types of support arrangements which will replace it, so it is important to invest time in developing the typology of support in a participatory manner. This maximises the potential for new reforms, once adopted, to be implemented in a manner that actually meets the needs of disabled people for flexible, human rights-compliant support arrangements that can be easily accessed and used for all the decisions that the persons concerned desire.

Different Approaches to the Provision of Support: From Natural Supports to Professionalism

The third element of the reforms which deserves attention is the difference in approaches regarding who can be recognised as a supporter. Most jurisdictions allow for a combination of approaches, enabling individuals to choose from among the people with whom they already have relationships of trust, as well as providing an option for the designation of an independent support person by a State body if the person needs support but cannot identify an individual to assist them. However, there is a large degree of variation in how the designation of supporters or representatives operates in practice. For example, in Ireland (Flynn, 2022) and Austria (Latimier, 2022), the State will not provide an independent support person, only an independent substitute decision-maker (decision-making representative or statutory representative) where there are no suitable family members or friends who can be appointed by the court. By contrast, in Colombia, a judge can appoint a personal defender from the Office of the Ombudsman to provide support if the person does not have anyone in their life who can provide this support (Ramos, 2020), but this cannot be done if the person concerned objects to having a supporter appointed (unlike in Ireland and Austria, where the representative can be appointed over the objections of the person concerned).

Legal frameworks that recognise the importance of naturally occurring supports are valuable, and these are rooted in the origins of supported decision-making as a concept and practice. They also reflect the social and cultural contexts of the jurisdictions which have adopted this approach, where families provide much of the support for disabled people in their day-to-day lives and can be crucial to supporting disabled people's autonomy and self-determination. However, lawmakers should not ignore the realities that many disabled people, especially those who have experienced segregation and institutionalisation, are without naturally occurring supports in their lives. The obligations placed on States in the General Comment include the facilitation and creation of support structures that people can then rely on if they wish to formally appoint supporters in legally binding agreements. This can be achieved in part by implementing other obligations under the CRPD, including enabling disabled people to live independently and be included in their communities. Careful monitoring will always be required to ensure that all supporters, including those provided by the State, honour their obligations to respect the individual's will and preferences and that they do not revert to substituted decision-making approaches.

Different jurisdictions have different responses to the idea of paid supporters exercising legal capacity. In Ireland, for example, an individual cannot appoint a staff member of a residential service where they live as their decision-making assistant or co-decision-maker (Flynn, 2022). This was intended to reduce conflicts of interest, where paid staff may have different responsibilities in their paid role compared to the role of supporting the person to have their will and preferences recognised. However, this approach assumes that any conflicts of interest that may arise among family and friends appointed to these roles can be more easily resolved than the conflicting obligations paid supporters may face. Moreover, the failure of the State to offer an alternative form of support beyond friends and family members means that many disabled people are not in a position to use these more flexible support arrangements and may end up in substituted decision-making systems with the appointment of a decision-making representative from the courts.

While conscious of the need to provide support options for people without naturally occurring support in their lives, activists have warned against the over-professionalisation of support to exercise legal capacity and the risks inherent in creating a new supported decision-making industry. The increasing professionalisation of support to exercise legal capacity risks changing the nature of the support provided, emphasising professional knowledge and expertise over the lived realities of disabled people who use this support, which could lead to a resurgence in the very kinds of paternalism that supported decision-making was intended to end. At the same time, we must recognise and develop systems to address conflicts of interest which arise between the person and their supporters, whether the supporters are independent professionals or friends and family members. Care should be taken to ensure that systems to address conflict are not themselves paternalistic in approach but are grounded in respect for the will and preferences of the person.

Different Approaches to Legal Recognition of Supports: Registration and Oversight Bodies

The final dimension I will consider regarding the application of Article 12 at the national level is the different approaches taken to the legal recognition of support arrangements. In most jurisdictions, support agreements need to be officially registered with a public body before they take legal effect or notarised by a person with specific authority to do so. When determining the best way forward for the legal recognition of supports, it is important to consider the financial and bureaucratic barriers that these may present to disabled people and their supporters. Requirements for online registration of support agreements, for example, will disadvantage many disabled people who experience the digital divide and those who do not have access to the technology required or assistance to use it while maintaining their right to privacy (Joint Committee on Children, Disability, Equality, Integration and Youth, 2022). Access to notaries public in many jurisdictions also presents a barrier, especially where notaries develop practices of requiring medical evidence of the person's capacity to create the agreement, even where this was not envisaged in the framework of the legislative reform.

In some jurisdictions, a new public body has been established to oversee the registration or legal recognition of support agreements, such as the Decision Support Service in Ireland (Flynn, 2021). In contrast, other jurisdictions have relied on existing structures, such as the Office of the Ombudsman in Austria and Colombia or notaries in Spain and Peru, who already have expertise in witnessing and approving official documents. Some jurisdictions have renamed and reformed previously existing structures to oversee this process; for example, the local and regional guardianship offices were renamed Adult Protection Offices in Austria's law reform (Latimier, 2022). As discussed above, when reforming existing structures, renaming is not sufficient to ensure the structural change necessary to achieve the obligations set out in Article 12 and General Comment 1.

The role of State bodies and the role of civil society organisations in implementing and overseeing human rights compliance of these new or reformed organisational structures is also important to consider. In some jurisdictions, such as Costa Rica, the State has not designated a specific public body to register support agreements or provide guidance to the public on how one should be created, leaving a gap which civil society organisations may attempt to fill (Marshall et al., 2023). Civil society organisations, including representative organisations of disabled people, are generally more accessible for those on the ground, and often have extensive knowledge of supported decision-making practices and can support peer learning and valuable exchange of practices (Browning et al., 2014). Nevertheless, the State must fulfil its obligations under Article 12 to create the conditions under which disabled people can access the support they may require in the exercise of their legal capacity and not simply delegate the entirety of this responsibility (without providing adequate resourcing and structures) to civil society organisations.

For more complex support arrangements, the resolution of conflicts between supporters or the appointment of a decision-maker in one of the 'hard cases' described above, most domestic law reforms have designated a court or tribunal to oversee the process. This approach can present some advantages in providing procedural safeguards for the respect of the person's rights, especially where free legal representation is provided alongside procedural accommodations necessary for the person concerned to participate effectively in legal proceedings (Flynn, 2021). However, access to courts is often expensive, time-consuming, and overly bureaucratic, resulting in many disabled people and their supporters being reluctant to engage with processes requiring court oversight. Moreover, the experience in several jurisdictions to date demonstrates that the courts' interpretations of the relevant legislative reforms are at times more conservative than the vision of disabled people and their supporters, who advocated for the reforms to be adopted (Ribot Igualada, 2023; Marshall et al., 2023).

From this brief overview, it is clear that many of the domestic legal capacity law reforms purporting to be Article 12 compliant have yet to achieve the standards actually established in General Comment 1. While the introduction of legally recognised mechanisms for supported decision-making has proliferated since the entry into force of the Convention, law reforms which actually abolish all forms of substituted decision-making prohibited by the General Comment are far rarer. It is worth reiterating that compliance with Article 12 cannot be achieved, in the view of the Committee, by simply introducing supported decision-making in law; substituted decision-making regimes must be fully abolished to ensure full human rights compliance. The different approaches represented among the domestic law reforms completed to date demonstrate that there are many different ways in which compliance with the Committee's interpretation of Article 12 could be achieved and reinforce the Committee's decision not to name any specific practice or legislative reform as being fully compliant with all of the requirements of the Convention.

Conclusion

The Committee's decision to set a high bar for full compliance with Article 12 in General Comment 1 will always be criticised by those who are more concerned with protecting the person from risk than supporting an individual's autonomy. However, with the clarity that the General Comment has provided, domestic lawmakers can no longer claim that there is no guidance on how the rights enumerated under Article 12 are to be achieved. Moreover, with growing examples of law reform, particularly from Latin America, that demonstrate what full compliance with these requirements could look like, it becomes more difficult for lawmakers to maintain their assertions that it is impossible for legal systems to move away from determinations of mental capacity in the designation of supports to enable the exercise of legal capacity.

Moving forward, a key consideration for grassroots activists and law reformers alike will be to remain steadfast in articulating what counts as support to exercise legal capacity and what does not. As outlined in the General Comment, support cannot be imposed over the person's objections, must rely on will and preference as the baseline for decisions, and cannot rely on cognitive tests (including functional assessments) of mental capacity to determine which form of support the person can use. By this criterion, only Peru and Colombia reached the threshold of compliance with the General Comment (Marshall et al., 2023). All the other jurisdictions considered in this chapter still provide for the appointment of representatives over the person's objections and/or rely on functional assessments of mental capacity to determine what supports a person can access. We must also continue to emphasise the Committee's position that the provision for supported decision-making agreements in law is not sufficient to ensure full compliance with Article 12 and continue to demand the repeal of all substituted decision-making regimes which violate the right to legal capacity of persons with disabilities. Since Article 12 is a civil and political right, it takes immediate effect (Committee on the Rights of Persons with Disabilities, 2014), and States cannot argue that by creating supports while maintaining substituted decision-making regimes, they are progressively realising this right.

Achieving full compliance with Article 12 in domestic law reform and the implementation of these reforms in practice remains a constant challenge, even in jurisdictions whose legal frameworks on their face comply with the requirements of the General Comment. It is only through the continued and concerted efforts of disabled people and their representative organisations, with the buy-in of key stakeholders, including parliamentarians, ministry officials, professional bodies, and the resourcing of support structures required to underpin new systems, that the true recognition in practice of the rights enshrined in Article 12 can hope to be achieved.

References

Arstein-Kerslake, A., & Flynn, E. (2016). The General Comment on Article 12 of the Convention on the Rights of Persons with Disabilities: A Roadmap for Equality Before the Law. *The International Journal of Human Rights, 20*(4), 471–490. https://doi.org/10.1080/13642987.2015.1107052

Australia, Combined second and third periodic reports submitted by Australia under article 35 of the Convention, due in 2018 CRPD/C/AUS/2-3 (2019).

Bach, M., & Espejo-Yaksic, N. (Eds.). (2023). Legal Capacity, Disability and Human Rights, Intersentia, paperback, xxiii378, 93.40€, ISBN: 978-1-83970-334-8.

Browning, M., Bigby, C., & Douglas, J. (2014). Supported Decision Making: Understanding How Its Conceptual Link to Legal Capacity Is Influencing the Development of Practice. *Research and Practice in Intellectual and Developmental Disabilities, 1*(1), 34–45. https://doi.org/10.1080/23297018.2014.902726

Canada, Combined second and third periodic reports submitted by Australia under article 35 of the Convention, due in 2020 CRPD/C/CAN/2-3 (2022).

Committee on the Rights of Persons with Disabilities, General Comment No. 1 – Article 12: Equal Recognition Before the Law CRPD/GC/1 (2014), corr.1 (2018).

Consideration of Reports Submitted by States Parties under Article 35 of the Convention: Concluding Observations, Tunisia, Committee on the Rights of Persons with Dis- abilities (CRPD), 5th Session, at 4, UN Doc. CRPD/C/TUN/CO/1 (11–15 April 2011).

Consideration of Reports Submitted by States Parties under Article 35 of the Convention: Concluding Observations, Spain, Committee on the Rights of Persons with Disabilities (CRPD), 6th Session, at 5, UN Doc. CRPD/C/ESP/CO/1 (19–23 September 2011).

Constantino Caycho, R. A. (2020). The Flag of Imagination: Peru's New Reform on Legal Capacity for Persons with Intellectual and Psychosocial Disabilities and the Need for New Understandings in Private Law. *The Age of Human Rights Journal, 14*, 155–180. https://doi.org/10.17561/tahrj.v14.5482

Constantino Caycho, R. A., & Bregaglio Lazarte, R. A. (2023). A Four-Speed Reform: A Typology for Legal Capacity Reforms in Latin American Countries. *Laws, 12*(3), 45. https://doi.org/10.3390/laws12030045

Flynn, E. (2021). Law, Language and Personhood: Disrupting Definitions of Legal Capacity. *Griffith Law Review, 30*(3), 374–394. https://doi.org/10.1080/10383441.2022.2035947

Flynn, E. (2022). The (Contested) Role of the Academy in Activist Movements for Legal Capacity Reform: A Personal Reflection. In M. Donnelly, R. Harding, & E. Tascıogliu (Eds.), *Supporting Legal Capacity in Socio-Legal Context*. Hart Publishing.

Flynn, E., & Arstein-Kerslake, A. (2017). State Intervention in the Lives of People with Disabilities: The Case for a Disability-Neutral Framework. *International Journal of Law in Context, 13*(1), 39–57. https://doi.org/10.1017/S1744552316000495

Freeman, M. C., et al. (2015). Reversing hard won victories in the name of human rights: a critique of the General Comment on Article 12 of the UN Convention on the Rights of Persons with Disabilities. The Lancet Psychiatry, 2.9: 844–850.

Ireland, Interpretative Declarations and Reservations upon Ratification of the United Nations Convention on the Rights of Persons with Disabilities. (2018, March 20). UNTS vol. 2515, p. 3.

Joint Committee on Children, Disability, Equality, Integration and Youth. (2022). Report on Pre Legislative Scrutiny of the Assisted Decision-Making (Capacity) Amendment Bill 2021 (Dublin: Houses of Oireachtas).

Latimier, C. (2022). *Legal Capacity and Supported Decision-Making: Lessons and Outcomes of Pilot Projects Implementing Article 12 of the United Nations Convention on the Rights of Persons with Disabilities*. University of Kent.

Marshall, P., Vásquez, P., Purán, V., & Godoy, L. (2023). Are We Closing the Gap? Reforms to Legal Capacity in Latin America in Light of the Convention on the Rights of Persons with Disabilities. *Vanderbilt Journal of. Transnational Law, 56*, 119.

Norway, Consideration of reports submitted by States parties under article 35 of the Convention Initial reports of States parties due in 2015 CRPD/C/NOR/1 (2015).

Plumb, A. (2015). UN Convention on the Rights of Persons with Disabilities: Out of the Frying Pan Into the Fire? Mental Health Service Users and Survivors Aligning with the Disability Movement. In *Madness, Distress and the Politics of Disablement* (pp. 183–198). Policy Press.

Ramos, S. H. (2020). Capacidad en Situación de Discapacidad: Análisis de la Ley 1996 de 2019. *Revista Latinoamericana en Discapacidad, Sociedad y Derechos Humanos, 4*(1), 60–82.

Ribot Igualada, J. (2023). The Reforms of Spanish Law on Legal Capacity and Supported Decision-Making for Persons with Disabilities. *Family & Law, 2023*(2), 1–22. https://doi.org/10.5553/FenR/.000060

Ruck Keene, A., Kane, N. B., Kim, S. Y., & Owen, G. S. (2023). Mental Capacity—Why Look for a Paradigm Shift? *Medical Law Review, 31*(3), 340–357. https://doi.org/10.1093/medlaw/fwac052

Szmukler, G., Daw, R., & Callard, F. (2014). Mental Health Law and the UN Convention on the Rights of Persons with Disabilities. *International Journal of Law and Psychiatry, 37*(3), 245–252. https://doi.org/10.1016/j.ijlp.2013.11.024

Szmukler, G. (2019). "Capacity", "best interests", "will and preferences" and the UN Convention on the Rights of Persons with Disabilities. *World Psychiatry, 18*(1), 34–41.
University of Cambridge, Cambridge Intellectual & Developmental Disabilities Research Group, Submission on the Draft General Comment on Article 12 of the Convention. (2014, January). http://www.ohchr.org/Documents/HRBodies/CRPD/GC/UniversityCambridgeGCArticle12.doc
United Nations Committee on the Rights of Persons with Disabilities (2014), General Comment 1 CRPD CRPD/GC/1.
Vasquez, A. (2021). The Potential of the Legal Capacity Law Reform in Peru to Transform Mental Health Provision. In M. A. Stein, F. Mahomed, V. Patel, & C. Sunkel (Eds.), *Mental Health, Legal Capacity, and Human Rights*. Cambridge University Press.

Open Access This chapter is licensed under the terms of the Creative Commons Attribution 4.0 International License (http://creativecommons.org/licenses/by/4.0/), which permits use, sharing, adaptation, distribution and reproduction in any medium or format, as long as you give appropriate credit to the original author(s) and the source, provide a link to the Creative Commons license and indicate if changes were made.

The images or other third party material in this chapter are included in the chapter's Creative Commons license, unless indicated otherwise in a credit line to the material. If material is not included in the chapter's Creative Commons license and your intended use is not permitted by statutory regulation or exceeds the permitted use, you will need to obtain permission directly from the copyright holder.

3

Legal Framework of the Accompanied Adult: Regime and Challenges in the Light of the CRPD

Inês Robalo

Abstract In this chapter, we describe the main features of the Portuguese legal framework for the accompaniment of adults with disabilities, its objectives, scope of application and general principles of necessity and subsidiarity. This regime seeks an individual response, with tailor-made measures which must be fitted into an accompanying legal regime. This legal framework respects the autonomy of will, especially in aspects relating to legal standing, procedural participation and the possibility of a mandate for future accompaniment. However, there are still aspects of this legal framework that need to be improved, essentially with a view to bringing it closer to the human rights model established by the United Nations Convention on the Rights of Persons with Disabilities.

Keywords Legal framework • Accompanied adult • Autonomy of will • CRPD • Human rights

---

I. Robalo (✉)
Prosecutor General's Office, Lisbon, Portugal
e-mail: ines.maria.robalo@pgr.pt

© The Author(s) 2026

P. Campos Pinto et al. (eds.), *Equal Rights, Equal Voices*, Palgrave Socio-Legal Studies,
https://doi.org/10.1007/978-3-032-05969-7_3

Brief Historical Background

Since the approval of the Portuguese Civil Code of 1966 (hereinafter CC), Portuguese civil law was in effect a legal model of incapacity for adults that had been unanimously considered for many years to be unsuited to the social and scientific reality and, above all, unsuited to the human rights model that the United Nations Convention on the Rights of Persons with Disabilities (hereinafter CRPD) came to implement or reinforce (Gomes, 2016)—reinforcement because the Portuguese Constitution already has specific guarantees of human rights and dignity.

In fact, the constitutional model for the defence of human rights, especially those classified as rights, freedoms and guarantees, already meant that the application of legal rules that conflict with those human rights must be interpreted and applied in such a way as to maximise their efficiency and respect the essential core of human dignity (Vítor, 2010).

In this context, especially after Portugal became bound by the CRPD (in 2009),[1] successive studies were carried out in preparation for the legislative change that was emerging.

The imperatives of the instruments of public international law to which Portugal was bound, in particular, the CRPD, were decisive for the (growing) recognition and effective protection of the rights of (adult) people with disabilities.

In broad terms, this is the background to the approval of Law no. 49/2018, 14 August, which aimed to create the legal framework (material law and procedural law) of the accompanied adult and to eliminate the institutes of *interdição/guardianship* and *inabilitação/curatorship*.

[1] The Convention was approved by the Resolution of the Portuguese Parliament no. 56/2009, of 07/30; ratified by Presidential Decree no. 71/2009, of 07/30. After the deposit of the instrument of ratification, the Convention came into force in Portugal on October 23, 2009.

The Objectives of the Accompanied Adult Regime

The accompanied adult legal regime thus emerged to respond to a new model for guaranteeing the rights of persons with disabilities.

It sought to provide a legal response to the basic principles established in the CRPD, namely, the general principle of "*Respect for inherent dignity, individual autonomy including the freedom to make one's own choices, and independence of persons*" [article 4 (a) of CRPD].

In these terms, the Portuguese legislator intended an individualised response to be given to the different conditions of the capacity of the adult, taking into account their specific support needs.

In the explanatory memorandum to the draft law that gave rise to Law 49/2018, it was written, in a promising way, that the intention was to adopt a "*model of accompaniment and not substitution, in which the impaired person is simply supported in the formation and externalisation of their will and not replaced in their will, which is in fact that of the representative*".

Protecting without incapacitating was the motto adopted by the authors of this legislative reform (Monteiro, 2018), designed to make the transition from the substitute decision-making model to the supported decision-making model. These were the main objectives of this legislative reform: *(i) primacy of the autonomy of the will; (ii) subsidiarity of judicial limitations on the capacity of adult persons; (iii) flexibility, based on the idea that each case is different; and (iv) speeding up procedures.*

This paradigm shift involves moving away from the simple declaration of incapacity. The aim is now to provide support to increase their autonomy and their ability to exercise their rights [cf. article 140(1) of the CC].

The Main Features of the Regime

Scope of Application

Article 138 of the CC (as amended by Law 49/2018) defines the scope of the accompanied adult regime, stating that "Adults who are unable, for reasons of health, disability or their behaviour, to fully, personally and consciously exercise their rights or fulfil their duties, benefit from the accompanying measures provided for in this Code".

This provision is in line with the provisions of the CRPD, when Article 12(3) states that the purpose of the intervention to promote the rights and protection of people with disabilities is "to provide access by persons with disabilities to the support they may require in exercising their legal capacity".

However, the wording of Article 138 reveals that the regime of the accompanied adult has not completely abandoned the medical model.

Firstly, Portuguese law continues to refer to health reasons, appealing to the concept of illness, when we know that the correct definition of disability under the CRPD is very far from that concept.

In fact, under the CRPD, disability should be understood as any obstacle found in a person's environment that makes it impossible for them to exercise their rights (and fulfil their duties) in a personal and autonomous way. As you can see, disability, seen from this perspective, is not something inherent to the person as such, but to the conditions they experience in their specific context, relating to barriers to the exercise of rights. It is a social construct or a circumstance in which they find themselves, as something in the environment that can be adjusted, improved, with a view to the dignified exercise of rights, in conditions of equality (United Nations, 2018).

On the other hand, the legal reference to *behaviour* appears, in our view, out of context, in light of the CRPD. It recalls the situations that could justify the old *inabilitação/curatorship*, which includes situations of prodigality (Gomes, 2020). However, the new paradigm seeks to move away from such definitions and ends up not defining which *behaviours* could justify the said *inability* to exercise rights. This is, therefore, a scope of application that remains legally undefined.

Necessity and Subsidiarity

Respect for proportionality guides any restriction on fundamental rights. This is stated in Article 18 of the Portuguese Constitution.

In defining the appropriate accompanying measures and, beforehand, in assessing the need for accompaniment, the principle of proportionality must be taken into account, in its threefold aspect: necessity, appropriateness and proportionality in the strict sense.

With this in mind, the Portuguese legislator introduced this guarantee of proportionality in Article 140(2) of the CC: "The measure does not take place whenever its objective is guaranteed through the general duties of co-operation and assistance that apply in the case".

In other words, it guarantees that there is only a place for judicial proceedings when the general duties of assistance are not sufficient to ensure the support the person needs. *General duties of co-operation and assistance* that the legislator has not defined and which, in our opinion, refer to social, housing (with autonomy), and accessibility assistance and support policies that the government is also responsible for implementing. The CRPD also obliges every contracting State to do this, in the general obligations set out in Article 4 and throughout the text that enshrines the various rights of persons with disabilities.

Returning to Article 140(2), in practice, whenever a person is familiarly and socially integrated and, as a result, is able to access all the support they need, no accompanying measures should be applied.

Therefore, the application of accompanying measures is governed by the principles of necessity and proportionality, which state that any measure should only be applied if its purpose cannot be achieved by another means that is less restrictive of the adult capacity.

However, when it came to defining the appropriate measure to apply, the legislator was not so clear in delimiting the parameters of proportionality.

Accompanying Measures and Restriction of Rights

Individualised Response

In defining the legal regime of accompaniment, the Portuguese legislator opted to define just one legal figure, which allows an individualised response to the different conditions and to the specific support needs of the adult.

This is also the direction taken by Article 12(4) of the CRPD, which states that measures relating to the exercise of legal capacity are proportional and tailored to the person's circumstances.

In these terms, the Portuguese legislator opted for the creation of an accompaniment model, whose measures would be flexible enough to adapt to each person's needs. That is why the first part of Article 145(2) of the CC, before the list of regimes for accompanying measures, states "according to each case". This adaptability to each case also has the virtue of safeguarding the principle of capacity.

However, the desired flexibility was not, in our opinion, sufficiently expressed in the legal text when listing the regimes applicable to the various accompanying measures, and much less so in practice, as can be seen from the data obtained and publicised as part of the EQUAL project.

Even so, from a procedural point of view, flexibility has been achieved by classifying the accompaniment legal procedure as, in part, a *non-contentious proceeding*. In line with this, the court decision is not limited to the initial request, as it also results from the substantive law, since Article 145(2) of the CC establishes that the court decides the accompaniment regime to be applied "regardless of what has been requested".

So, in order to effectively adapt the accompanying measures to each case, the identification of the obstacles that constitute disability must always be accompanied by the identification of the support that will allow to overcome them, supporting the person in exercising their rights. And this identification of the necessary support does not, in our view, simply involve identifying the most appropriate legal support system. This legal regime will be the box or basket into which the support can be placed in the judicial decision.

Therefore, the aims of the accompaniment—the well-being, empowerment and autonomy of the accompanied adult—will not be achieved by simply identifying one or more accompanying measures. In order to get there, the court will have to identify the specific support that a person needs at that specific moment in their life. This would be a suitable method for constructing the so-called *tailor-made suit*.

Accompanying Legal Regimes

In order to adapt the accompanying measure to each specific situation, Article 145 of the CC establishes the following regimes:

(a) Exercise of parental responsibilities or the means to fulfil them, depending on the circumstances;
(b) General representation or special representation with an express indication, in this case, of the categories of acts for which it is necessary;
(c) Total or partial administration of assets;
(d) Prior authorisation to carry out certain acts or categories of acts;
(e) Interventions of other kinds, duly explained.

Firstly, the Portuguese legislator has not abolished legal regimes that fall under the substitute decision-making model. On the contrary, the first paragraphs and most of the regimes to which they all refer fit precisely into that model. In fact, applying the equivalent regime to parental responsibilities means putting someone else—the accompanying person/representative—in charge of deciding for the accompanied adult, in their place. This is a sign that should be totally avoided, since equating the form of support for persons with disabilities in exercising their rights with the same means applicable to children is equivalent, even if symbolically, to make children of adult persons, which constitutes an assault on their dignity and fundamental rights.

So, the semantics used in the first two paragraphs, in particular the term *representation*, already reveals the model set out here, and the applicable regime leaves even more certainty: Article 145(4) of the CC states that legal representation follows the guardianship regime. There is, therefore, no doubt that there are few differences between the application of the previous *interdição / guardianship* and the current general representation.

Total or partial property administration regimes also fall under the substitute decision-making model. In effect, these regimes mean that it will be the accompanying person who will administer the property of the adult in their place (totally or partially) and not the accompanied adult, with the assistance or even prior authorisation (depending on the value, for example) of the accompanying person.

Article 145(5) of the CC also mandates the application of Articles 1967 et seq. of the same Code to the total or partial administration of assets, with the necessary adaptations. These provisions derive precisely from the guardianship regime.

As a result, of the five regimes listed above, three do not provide the person most closely supervised with any decision-making autonomy, nor do they promote their empowerment for this purpose. On the contrary, they put someone else in charge of deciding their life's affairs in their place.

In fact, the only legal regimes that potentially fit into the supported decision-making model are those provided for in points (d) and (e). And we say potentially because, in fact, the law, by openly establishing interventions of other kinds, does not establish how these interventions translate into the exercise of rights and fulfilment of duties by the accompanied adult. Although it would be necessary for the law to establish an open system of support, precisely in order to be able to accommodate the specific needs of each accompanied adult, the truth is that the term interventions includes both acts of substitution and acts of effective support. It would be different if the law established support of a different kind, thus unequivocally pointing to support or assistance measures, and not substituting decision-making measures.

Authorisation, on the other hand, gives the accompanied adult the opportunity for self-determination, even if it is limited, in the last act or in its implementation, to the authorisation of the accompanying person. In this sense, "the authorisation of the accompanying person only serves to reinforce the will, in those cases where there is not an absolute absence of self-determination" (Barbosa, 2020).[2]

The list of legal regimes is apparently ordered gradually: from the most severe regimes, from the perspective of representation, to the least restrictive and closest to true assistance.

The accompanying measures of representation are, in fact, the most restrictive of capacity, meaning that the person who benefits from it is replaced by their accompanying person, who is, in fact, a representative (in no way different from a guardian). And these accompanying measures subject to the regime of general representation continue to be, to a large extent, the most applied, in a percentage that exceeds 80 per cent, according to the data collected, by sampling (in three court counties), as part of the EQUAL Project. Still, the special representation will be less restrictive than the general representation, since the representation regime will only apply to certain aspects of adult life.

So, despite the objectives mentioned above and the imperatives of the CRPD, the truth is that Portuguese law has not yet adopted a legal regime that is truly or totally adept at the supported decision-making model.

In fact, contrary to what the legislator seems to have intended, any legal provision determines that the measures to be applied should preferably be measures of effective assistance. Despite the fact that Article 145(1) of the CC establishes that accompaniment is limited to what is necessary, the truth is that it does not expressly establish that measures of representation should be applied exceptionally—an express determination which, in our opinion, would be decisive in guaranteeing effective respect for the principle of proportionality.

Restriction of Personal Rights

Article 147(1) of the CC states that "The exercise by the accompanied adult of personal rights and the conclusion of ordinary business transactions are free, unless otherwise provided by law or court decision".

---

[2] Free translation by author.

As a result, the restriction on the exercise of personal rights and the ability to enter into ordinary business is exceptional—exceptionality that already results both from the aforementioned Article 18 of the Constitution and from the CRPD itself.

And once again emphasised: the exceptional nature of the restriction on the exercise of personal rights (and on the ability to enter into ordinary business transactions) derives from a fundamental principle of persons' capacity, clearly defined in Article 12 of the CRPD, as well as the fundamental principle and pillar of our legal system: respect for the dignity of the human person (cf. Articles 1, 18 and 26 of the Portuguese Constitution).

Therefore, the exceptional nature of the restriction requires special justification from a procedural point of view. The restriction of personal rights and the ability to carry out everyday business, as well as the request for specific measures, must always be based on specific facts that justify it, as it is also clear from the final part of Article 892(1)(a) of the Portuguese Civil Code of Procedure (hereinafter: CCP).

It is not enough to infer from a diagnosis of dementia, for example, that the person is unable to decide where and with whom to live. The fact that there are certain limitations, particularly on an intellectual level, to the free and conscious making of certain decisions does not prevent persons with disabilities from freely expressing their preferences. And their preference to live with those with whom they feel the strongest emotional ties or where they feel most comfortable should indeed weigh heavily in the choice, even if the choice cannot be made exclusively on the basis of that will or preference (Martín, 2011).

In the same way that it is unreasonable for an adult in their eighties to see their right to procreate and give birth limited on a merely formal - more like formalistic - level.

What is more, the very legal provision limiting the right to procreate is highly questionable, since this right is, at best, the biological expression of an instinct whose legal limitation is not only fallacious but also artificial. In addition, it clearly violates the human rights and dignity of persons with disabilities.

Once again, only by getting to know that a specific person will we be able not only to adapt the accompanying measure to their needs but also to limit the restriction of rights to what, in fact, has a concrete factual exceptional basis in their life circumstances and capacity.

However, in too many cases, adults see their rights curtailed more severely than children, who are recognised as having the capacity to enter into minor everyday business within the scope of their natural capacity (see Article 127(1)(b) of the CC).

Finally, it should be noted that, in line with the CRPD, persons with disabilities retain ownership of their rights, and the decision limiting their ability to exercise their rights may be, in exceptional cases, a kind of way of protecting them (Vivas-Tesón, 2020).

Respect for the Autonomy of the Will

The legal regime of the accompanied adult also determines that the adult beneficiary is no longer the (mere) object of the decision but an active participating subject.

Article 12(4) of the CRPD establishes guarantees of respect for the autonomy of the will of persons with disabilities, safeguarding that the person's will and preferences are free of conflict of interest and undue influence. Here, as well as other aspects of the regime, Article 12 must be an interpretative light of this legal regime (Vítor, 2020). When applying this legal regime, the adult's will and preferences should be taken into account.

Therefore, persons with disabilities who benefit from accompanying measures must be given an effective voice, both in the process and more broadly, in the application of the measures themselves. It should be noted that not only the accompanying measures themselves must contribute to strengthening autonomy, but existing autonomy must also be respected, valued and exercised.

From a procedural perspective, Article 13 of the CRPD specifically enshrines the right to *effective access to justice for persons with disabilities on an equal basis with others*—which means that the necessary procedural adaptations must be made so that participation takes place under equal conditions.

Legal Standing

Respect for the will of the beneficiary is evident from the outset in their legal standing to bring about the action. Any other person, apart from the beneficiary themselves and with the exception of the Public Prosecutor's Office, will need the beneficiary's authorisation to judicially require an accompanying measure (cf., Article 141 of the CC).

The Public Prosecutor's Office has been granted special *legitimacy ad causam*, in which the legislator dispenses with the beneficiary's authorisation, insofar as it considers, in accordance with the statutory attributions, that the Public Prosecutor's Office acts to defend and promote the rights of vulnerable adults. As such, public prosecutors cannot exclude the adult from the decision-making process and must recognise the right to be heard in the phase in which the need for accompaniment is assessed and, as such, bring the action.

In other words, the legal standing of the Public Prosecutor's Office should not exclude the adult from this initial decision-making process.

In order for any other claimant to ask the court to apply for accompanying measures, it is necessary for the beneficiary to authorise it (Article 141(1) of the CC).

Article 141(2) of the CC states that "the court may override the beneficiary's authorisation when, in view of the circumstances, the beneficiary is unable to give it freely and knowingly, or when it considers that there are reasonable grounds for doing so". First, it should be pointed out that this last part, in the sense of the possibility of the existence of justifiable grounds for the court to override the beneficiary's authorisation, weakens what would be the initial strength of the autonomy of the adult beneficiary's will. This is a legal provision that, in our view, is still a remnant of a certain paternalism in the so-called protection of adults, considering that—given the use of the disjunctive expression *or*—it does not seem to depend on the impossibility of a free and conscious decision by the adult, but rather on a reasoned decision by the judge, which seems to us not be in harmony with either Article 12 or Article 13 of the Convention. Either the person is capable of giving their authorisation freely and knowingly, or they are not, and only in this case should their authorisation be superseded. If the adult is capable of giving their consent freely and knowingly, and if they don't, there are, in our view, no good reasons for the court to override their consent. To believe otherwise is, in our opinion, to take away decision-making power and drastically reduce the autonomy of the will that should be recognised for persons with disabilities.

On the other hand, this authorisation is a question of legal standing. In other words, it is a procedural prerequisite for bringing an action. What is particularly relevant is when this authorisation, and if necessary, when it needs to be granted, should take place procedurally. As it is a procedural prerequisite for the regularity of the action, it should be checked right at its start.

However, in order to facilitate the procedure and avoid duplication of steps, such as hearing the beneficiary and carrying out medical expertise to assess their capacity to decide, it is very often relegated to the final decision. This procedural practice, in our opinion, may jeopardise the effective exercise of autonomy of the will.

When the application for accompanying measures is submitted by any applicant other than the beneficiary adult or the Public Prosecutor's Office, the first step should always be to hear the adult. At that point, the beneficiary's free and conscious decision to give their authorisation would be assessed. If this is given, the process will continue. If there are doubts about the beneficiary's ability to make a free and informed decision, the preliminary phase of the procedure would continue with a view to possibly override the authorisation.

Procedural Participation

Law 49/2018 made it compulsory for the beneficiary to be heard.

Article 898(1) of the CPC states that the hearing must be personal and direct. This legal determination points out the preference for a personal hearing. In our opinion, it is also important to take into account the diverse communication methods of persons with disabilities (United Nations, 2018).

The same provision states that the hearing "aims to ascertain their situation and decide on the most appropriate accompanying measures". In this sense, it would be imperative that instead of the questions about, for example, the seasons or mathematical calculations, questions were asked that would help to find out about the daily lives of the adult being heard, who supports them, and what support they believe is necessary for them to exercise their rights.

On the other hand, Article 898(2) states that "the questions shall be put by the judge, with the assistance of the applicant, the beneficiary's representatives and the (medical) expert, if appointed". Once again, this seems to be established from the perspective of the judge and not the adult, and reflects the medical model.

The law does not expressly provide for reasonable accommodation, in particular, the presence of a specialised technician to play the role of mediator or communication facilitator.

On the other hand, the fact that the law expressly establishes the presence of an expert—in practice, invariably a doctor—is a clear sign that it is still almost exclusively the responsibility of the doctor to assess the adult's capacity and the most appropriate accompanying measures.

Although the law does not expressly say so, the obligation to have a hearing must be reflected in an effective guarantee that the adult participates in the decision-making process on considering the accompanying measures needed and on choosing the accompanying person. As is easy to understand from the path traced in this chapter so far, a mere hearing with a questionnaire similar to the one used in the old *interdição / guardianship* processes is not enough to guarantee the effective active participation of the adult.

In order to guarantee this active participation, it will be necessary, in most situations, to adopt the necessary procedural adaptations, which means reasonable accommodation (United Nations, 2014). In this regard, it is important to emphasise that since disability is based on the obstacles arising from the person's interaction with the environment, the obstacles or difficulties in accessing justice and effectively participating in the process inevitably contribute to accentuating the disability.

One of the obstacles to effective communication is the fact that the hearing takes place in a courtroom, with all the formalism that inevitably goes with it, without the adult having been previously interviewed, without being given time and opportunity to integrate and find out about the purpose of the hearing and without the effective support of a trusted person.

To facilitate communication, one of the most important supports will be the presence of a trusted person and of a specialised technician to facilitate and mediate communication. This facilitator has, for example, been legally provided for in Spain by Law 8/2021 and Royal Decree 191/2023.

This facilitator should be able to speak to the adult before the event, to explain its purpose, where it will take place, who will be present and what is expected or what the purpose is.

The presence of a facilitator or specialised technician does not replace or exclude the right of the adult to be accompanied by someone they trust. This presence and support will contribute to lower levels of anxiety, greater security and, as such, a greater ability to communicate with the court.

The presence of this trusted person and their choice should be the sole decision of the adult, and they should not be constrained to the presence of a person who, even if they are close to them, is imposed by the court.

Another of the most important adaptations is to hold the hearing in as informal an environment as possible and using easy language, accessible to anyone.

It will be necessary to take into account the needs of the adult in order to feel integrated, understand the purpose of the hearing and be able to express themselves. As the UN General Comment No. 6 (2018) on non-discrimination and equality says, "Reasonable accommodation is an intrinsic part of the immediately applicable duty of non-discrimination in the context of disability".

Finally, this hearing procedure gives decision-makers the opportunity to get a direct insight into the person with disability and their relationship with those accompanying them during the procedure. This will also allow them to better assess the appropriateness of the measure(s) to be applied and that of the accompanying person.

This is a central theme of this regime, since we believe that respect for the autonomy of the will is a guarantee of human dignity.

Mandate for Future Accompaniment

Another aspect of the regime that is a sign of respect for the autonomy of the will is the mandate with a view to accompaniment provided for in Article 156 of the CC. It is possible for adults to establish in advance by whom and how they want to be supported or represented in the event of disability or impairment.

The law only states that "the mandate follows the general regime and specifies the rights involved and the scope of any representation, as well as any other elements or conditions of exercise, and is freely revocable by the principal".

Thus, it did not establish any kind of registration or formality, nor did it determine how such a mandate becomes effective and begins to produce effects. In other words, whether for this purpose, it would be necessary to verify the adult's impairment or the need for effective accompaniment.

Paragraph 3 of the same provision states that "at the time the order for accompaniment is made, the court shall take advantage of the mandate, in whole or in part, and shall take it into account when defining the scope of protection and appointing the accompanying person".

So, both this provision and the entire design of the regime point towards adult's will and preferences being taken into account. And even if the adult is currently not able to express their preferences fully and completely, it can be drawn from sedimented life preferences—the values and preferences expressed and sedimented throughout life or drawn from their behaviour, including when it comes to choosing the accompanying person.

Moreover, the legal regime attaches importance to prior or presumed expressions of the will, including for the purposes of revoking the mandate for future accompaniment (see Article 156(4) of the CC).

Expertise

Article 899(1) of the CCP establishes the object and purpose of the expertise carried out in this type of procedure, with a view to specifying "whenever possible, the condition from which the beneficiary suffers, its consequences, the probable date of its onset and the advisable means of support and treatment".

Although the compulsory nature of medical expertise is not established, it is quite common in practice and is a clear sign to us that the medical model is still in force in these proceedings, as opposed to the human rights model.

Without denying the importance of an expert medical judgement, when necessary, what we want to highlight is the continued central role of medical diagnosis and also the temptation to transfer responsibility for judging the necessity and suitability of accompanying measures to the medical expert.

On the contrary, the CRPD obliges States' parties to implement the human rights model, where diagnosis loses its central role and where the judge is required to apply a personalised measure with situational content. Therefore, rather than a mere technical scientific judgement, in order to define the appropriate measures, "the beneficiary's environment, personality, personal situation and relational life will have to be assessed" (Ribeiro, 2020). This, in our opinion, can be achieved not only through a report or social information but also through a direct perception of the adult and their relationship with those accompanying them.

Therefore, magistrates must "take on a proactive procedural management activity centred on identifying the subjective assumptions and, fundamentally, taking stock of the beneficiary's needs" (Ribeiro, 2020).

Conclusion

As we have seen, the CRPD recognises in Article 12 that all persons with disabilities have full legal capacity. And it is from this essential assumption that any application and interpretation of the regime of the adult accompanied must start.

In fact, it is the failure to recognise the legal capacity of persons with disabilities that leads to the restriction of personal rights, such as reproductive rights, or simply the right to decide where to live.

Thus, legal capacity should not be confused with mental capacity (United Nations, 2014), which in turn will depend on numerous factors that determine the individual's resources for free and conscious decision-making.

The new paradigm is based on a fundamental assumption of respect for difference and acceptance of people with disabilities as part of human diversity, with the "demand for respect and the right to be respected" and the recognition of the right to autonomy and self-determination for anyone, on equal terms (Albuquerque & Paz, 2016, pp. 31–32).

A final note to remember is that the effective implementation of the human rights model depends on an interdisciplinary and integrated response between the various entities with responsibility and intervention in this matter.

References

Albuquerque, J. P. R. d., & Paz, M. M. A. d. (2016). Adultos-idosos dependentes ou especialmente vulneráveis: aspectos da protecção penal e civil. *Revista Do Ministério Público, 146*, 9–46.

Barbosa, M. M. (2020). O regime do acompanhamento: da incapacidade à capacidade? *O Novo Regime Do Maior Acompanhado*, 165–187. https://doi.org/10.47907/livro/2022/Maior_Acompanhado/Cap07

Gomes, J. C. (2016). Constitucionalismo, Deficiência Mental e Discapacidade: um apelo aos Direitos. *Revista Julgar, 29*, 119–151.

Gomes, J. C. (2020). Os direitos humanos e o maior (des)acompanhado: causas e medidas de capacitação. *Revista Julgar, 41*, 49–76.

Martín, M. T. M. (2011). La Convención Internacional sobre los derechos de las Personas com Discapacidad como nuevo prescriptor de las legislaciones internas. Examen y Análisis del Artículo 19 de la Convención y su alcance, extensión e intensidade en España. Correspondencias y carências. *Revista de Derecho UNED, 9*, 49–76.

Monteiro, A. P. (2018). Das incapacidades ao maior acompanhado - Breve apresentação da Lei n.o 49/2018. *Revista de Legislação e de Jurisprudência, y148, 4013*, 87–107. https://gestlegal.pt/loja/revista-de-legislacao-e-de-jurisprudencia-ano-148-o-n-o-4013/

Ribeiro, G. R. (2020). O instituto do maio acompanhado à luz da Convenção de Nova Iorque e dos Direitos Fundamentais. *Colóquio: O Novo Regime Do Maior Acompanhado*, 319–379.

United Nations. (2014). *General Comment No. 1 - Article 12: Equal Recognition Before the Law.* https://www.ohchr.org/en/documents/general-comments-and-recommendations/general-comment-no-1-article-12-equal-recognition-1

United Nations. (2018). *General Comment No.6 on Equality and Non-Discrimination.* https://docs.un.org/en/CRPD/C/GC/6

Vítor, P. T. (2010). Capacidade e incapacidades: respostas do ordenamento jurídico português e o artigo 12.o da Convenção dos Direitos das Pessoas com Deficiência. *Revista Sociedade e Trabalho, 39*, 39–55.

Vítor, P. T. (2020). O maior acompanhado à luz do kartigo 12.o da CDPD. *Revista Julgar, 41*, 23–47.

Vivas-Tesón, I. (2020). La aplicación de la Conventión de Nueva York en España: una década de aciertos y desaciertos. *Colóquio: O Novo Regime Do Maior Acompanhado*, 7–56.

Open Access This chapter is licensed under the terms of the Creative Commons Attribution 4.0 International License (http://creativecommons.org/licenses/by/4.0/), which permits use, sharing, adaptation, distribution and reproduction in any medium or format, as long as you give appropriate credit to the original author(s) and the source, provide a link to the Creative Commons license and indicate if changes were made.

The images or other third party material in this chapter are included in the chapter's Creative Commons license, unless indicated otherwise in a credit line to the material. If material is not included in the chapter's Creative Commons license and your intended use is not permitted by statutory regulation or exceeds the permitted use, you will need to obtain permission directly from the copyright holder.

4

Realising the Right to Legal Capacity in Portugal

Paula Campos Pinto, Patrícia Neca, and Teresa Janela Pinto

Abstract This chapter presents the main results of the EQUAL project. A total of 747 legal rulings were analysed to assess what has changed and what has remained the same in the content of court decisions regarding legal capacity in the country. Taking a sociology of human rights perspective [Frezzo, *The Sociology of Human Rights*. Polity Press (2015); Pinto, *The Oxford Handbook of the Sociology of Human Rights* (pp. 175–194). Oxford University Press (2023)], the discussion on barriers to change was expanded with the cross-examination of the 31 interviews with key stakeholders. Finally, formal and informal barriers to agency and self-determination were further explored through four focus groups conducted with 19 persons with intellectual and psychosocial disabilities who have had their rights restricted. The triangulation of all these data allowed an

P. Campos Pinto (✉) • P. Neca • T. J. Pinto
Observatory on Disability and Human Rights and Interdisciplinary Centre on Gender Studies, Institute of Social and Political Sciences, University of Lisbon, Lisbon, Portugal
e-mail: mppinto@edu.ulisboa.pt; pneca@iscsp.ulisboa.pt; teresajpinto@iscsp.ulisboa.pt

© The Author(s) 2026

P. Campos Pinto et al. (eds.), *Equal Rights, Equal Voices*, Palgrave Socio-Legal Studies,
https://doi.org/10.1007/978-3-032-05969-7_4

in-depth understanding of the potentialities and limitations to the implementation of Article 12 of the Convention on the Rights of Persons with Disabilities (CRPD) in Portugal.

Keywords Legal capacity • CRPD • Intellectual and psychosocial disabilities • Portugal

Introduction

This chapter draws on the findings of the EQUAL project, '*Equality before the law and the right to self-determination of persons with intellectual and psychosocial disabilities*', a large-scale study conducted in Portugal between 2022 and 2023, which aimed to explore the challenges, barriers and opportunities surrounding the implementation of a legislative reform (Law 49/2018) aimed at transposing the standards of Article 12 of the CRPD into national law. The EQUAL project adopted a sociology of human rights lens (Frezzo, 2015; Pinto, 2023) and a mixed-methods approach, involving quantitative and qualitative data. First, we analysed 747 court decisions issued under the new Accompanied Adult Regime, gathered during the first four years of implementation of this law, in three judicial districts in Portugal: Lisbon (for an urban area), Viana do Castelo (for a semi-urban) and Évora (for a rural area). In addition, 31 semi-structured interviews with key stakeholders (judges, prosecutors, medical experts, disability service providers and families) and focus groups with 19 people with intellectual and psychosocial disabilities were carried out. The main findings of this study are presented below:

Overview of Court Rulings

As detailed in Chap. 3 in this book, under the new Accompanied Adult Regime, the courts may establish different types of support measures: general representation or special representation, in the latter case with the list of acts where such special representation is needed. Although these terms are not explicitly defined in the law, *general representation* is understood as a measure that restricts the exercise of rights to a greater extent than *special representation*.

Sample and Analytical Procedure

To identify trends and patterns in the implementation of the Regime of the Accompanied Adult during the first three years after the law's passage (from 10 February 2019 to 10 February 2023), this study specifically focused on which type of accompanying measures—general or special representation—were most frequently applied to persons with disabilities aged 18–55 years.

The research team did not assess the rulings directly, but the Prosecutor General's Office (a partner in the project) provided the following information on the court rulings ($N = 747$) analysed: judicial district of the court ruling (*Évora*, *Lisboa*, and *Viana do Castelo*), sex of the beneficiary (*male* or *female*), age of the beneficiary (*18–29, 30–45*; *46–55*), type of accompanying measure ruled (*general* or *special*), and, if applicable, personal rights removed (*right to make a will*; *reproductive rights and right to exercise parental responsibilities* (including through adopting a child); *right to marry or to be in a common-law partnership*; *right to choose a place of residence/mobility rights; right to conduct business*; *right to decide on issues related to medical care*; *right to choose a profession*; *right to vote*; and *right to access game rooms*). It also provided information on the disability of the beneficiary, as indicated in the ruling. As a wide range of medical labels were listed, the research team grouped them into six categories: *severe intellectual disability*; *mild or moderate intellectual disability*; *psychosocial disability*; *double diagnosis (involving both intellectual and psychosocial disabilities)*; and *various types of disability*. The category *various types of disability* captured a diversity of diagnoses and labels, which ranged from very specific (e.g. 'Metachromatic Leukodystrophy') to vague (e.g. 'Developmental Disorder') and even outdated terms (e.g. 'Deaf-Mute'), but without specifying the severity of the impairment. Descriptive statistics were conducted using SPSS, with chi-square tests or Fisher's exact tests applied to examine associations between the variables.

Sociodemographic Information

Of the 747 rulings analysed, 61.2% (*n* = 457) of the beneficiaries were male and 38.8% (*n* = 290) were female. Furthermore, 65.5% (*n* = 489) were from the district of Lisbon, 21.2% (*n* = 158) from Viana do Castelo and 13.4% (*n* = 100) from Évora. In all the districts, most of the rulings involved men: 62.4% in Lisbon, 59% in Évora, and 58.9% in Viana do Castelo. Regarding the age of the beneficiaries, 45% (*n* = 336) were aged between 18 and 29 years, 26.2% (*n* = 196) were aged between 30 and 45 years, and 28.8% (*n* = 215) were aged between 46 and 55 years.

As for the type of disability, more than half of the rulings (54.5%; *n* = 407) were classified as 'various types of disability'. In turn, in 16.3% (*n* = 122) of the rulings, the beneficiaries were people with 'psychosocial disabilities', followed by cases of 'severe intellectual disability' (*n* = 108; 14.5%), 'mild and/or moderate intellectual disability' (*n* = 101; 13.5%) and 'double diagnosis' (*n* = 9; 1.2%).

Accompanying Measures Applied: Evolution Over Time (2019–2023)

In 82.5% (*n* = 616) of the court rulings across the three districts, the judge decided on *general representation* (Fig. 4.1), that is, a more severe form of substitute decision-making measure, where an accompanying person/representative makes decisions for the beneficiary.

While general representation remained the predominant accompanying measure in all the three districts studied, it is noteworthy that its application has been decreasing over time. As shown in Fig. 4.2, in the court decisions issued between February 2019 and February 2022 (*n* = 528), 85.2% of the rulings assigned powers of *general representation* to the accompanying person/representative (similar to the previous guardianship regime [*interdição*]). However, in the most recent court decisions (issued between February 2022 and February 2023; *N* = 211), it was found that only 78.7% assigned general representation powers to the accompanying person/representative, and these differences were statistically significant (*p* = 0.037).

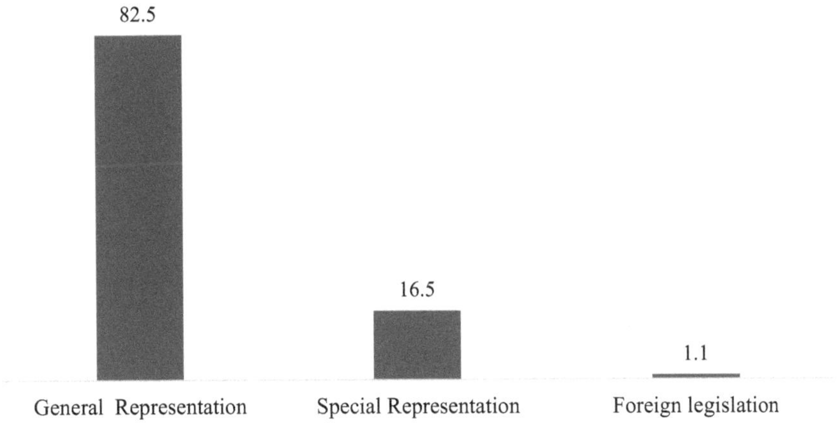

Fig. 4.1 Type of accompanying measures applied (2019–2023; N = 747; %). Source: Data provided by the Prosecutor General's Office (Portugal) upon request and processed by the EQUAL project team

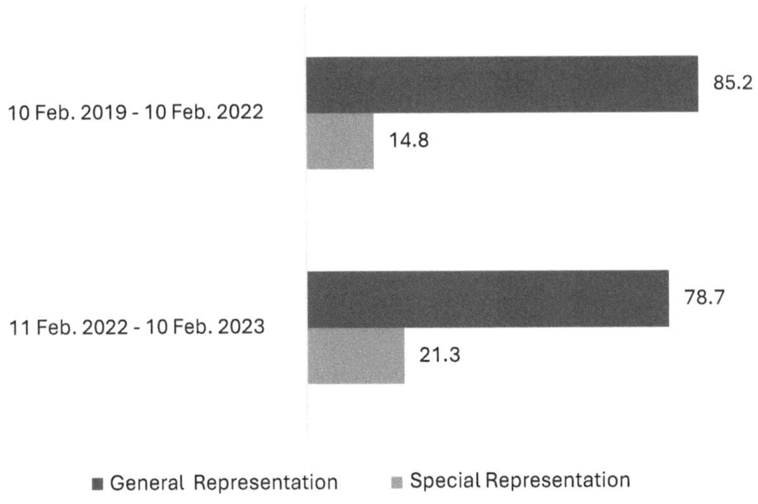

Fig. 4.2 Evolution of the accompanying measures applied (N = 739; %). Source: Data provided by the Prosecutor General's Office (Portugal) upon request and processed by the EQUAL project team; Note: Exclusion of eight cases of foreign legislation (N = 739)

Accompanying Measures Applied Differ Based on the Type of Disability

Depending on the type of disability considered, the analysis also revealed different patterns of the accompanying measures applied: general representation or special representation. Thus, *general representation* was associated with rulings involving people with 'severe intellectual disability' or 'various types of disability', while *special representation* was associated with cases of 'psychosocial disability' and 'mild or moderate intellectual disability'. These differences were statistically significant: ($\chi 2$ (4739) = 37.398, p = <0.001). In summary, the latter seems to face fewer restrictions.

Restriction of Personal Rights

According to Article 147 of the Civil Code, beneficiaries of the accompanying measures may freely exercise their personal rights and carry out ordinary business transactions unless stated otherwise in the court decision. Nevertheless, of the 747 rulings examined, only 10% ($N = 75$) did not mention any restriction on the exercise of personal rights, while 90% ($N = 672$) imposed restrictions on at least one personal right, as shown in Fig. 4.3.

In 55.3% ($N = 413$) of the cases, the court decided to deprive the beneficiary of the accompanying measures from exercising five or more (up to a maximum of 11) personal rights (Fig. 4.3). In only 9.8% ($n = 73$) of the rulings, only one personal right was restricted. This result contrasts with the objectives and spirit of the Convention, which call for the recognition of legal capacity for all people, as well as with Law 49/2018, which states that the limitation of personal rights should be the exception and not the rule.

A more detailed analysis of the rights supressed considering the rulings where at least one personal right was limited (90%; $n = 672$) shows that the most frequently personal rights removed were (Fig. 4.4) the right to make a will ($n = 632$; 94%), reproductive rights/right to exercise parental responsibilities ($n = 538$; 80.1%), right to marry or to be in a

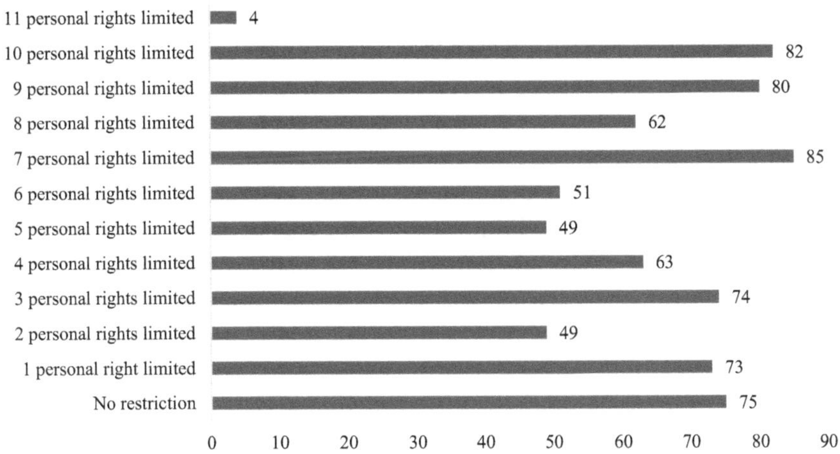

Fig. 4.3 Limitations on personal rights ($N = 747$; N). Source: Data provided by the Prosecutor General's Office (Portugal) upon request and processed by the EQUAL project team

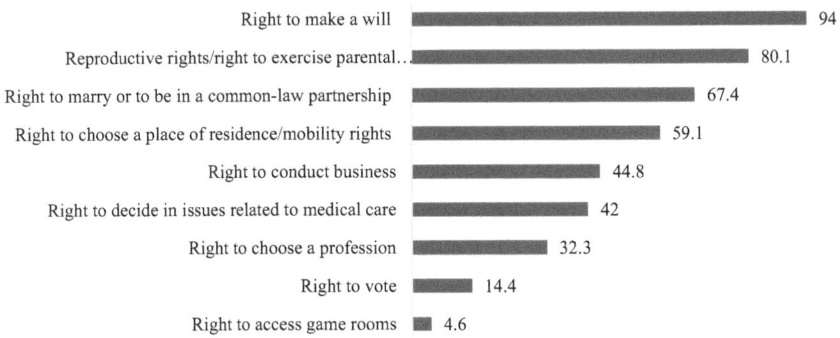

Fig. 4.4 Types of personal rights restricted ($n = 672$; %). Source: Data provided by the Prosecutor General's Office (Portugal) upon request and processed by the EQUAL project team. Note: the analysis includes rulings with restriction of at least one personal right ($n = 672$). Reproductive rights/right to exercise parental responsibilities (*) include 'Reproductive rights', 'Parenting', 'Exercising Parental Responsibilities' and 'Adopting'

common-law partnership (n = 453; 67.4%) and the right to choose a place of residence/mobility rights (n = 397; 59.1%).

It is worth noting that the personal rights that have more implications for third parties, such as the 'right to make a will' (for its possible damage to family assets and heritage) and 'reproductive rights/exercise of parental responsibilities' (for its potential consequences for the reproduction of disability itself, as well as childcare provision), take on particular significance in this context. In other words, rights related to financial matters, as well as reproductive and marital rights, are the most frequently limited personal rights. This may be a strong indication of the courts' understanding of disability as a medical, vulnerable and irrational condition, which requires protection as well as containment and control (Foucault, 1976), as it may constitute a danger or a burden to families, community and society. As already highlighted in Chap. 2, these restrictions, however, contradict Article 12 and fail to recognise full legal capacity.

Interviews with Key Stakeholders

This section draws on 31 semi-structured interviews conducted nationwide with key stakeholders involved in the implementation of law 49/2018, including judges, prosecutors and bailiffs (n = 8), technical directors and professionals from support services for persons with intellectual and psychosocial disabilities (n = 9), experts responsible for medico-legal and social assessments (n = 7); and family members of persons with intellectual or psychosocial disabilities (n = 7). These interviews aimed to capture diverse perspectives and experiences, providing a comprehensive understanding of the law's application in practice. The following topics were addressed in the interviews: socio-demographic information, the participants' role in the implementation of the law, general perception of Law 49/2018, positive aspects, constraints and challenges in implementing the law, suggestions and recommendations for improving its implementation, and views on disability. All the interviews were fully transcribed and subjected to thematic analysis (Braun et al., 2019) that enabled the identification of the themes or topics addressed. In what follows, we present and discuss those themes.

A 'custom-made suit'

The new Accompanied Adult Regime is recognised by most stakeholders as a significant advancement, aligned with a rights-based approach and the commitments established in the CRPD. One of its most valued aspects is the flexibility it provides, allowing support measures to be tailored to the specific needs of each individual, which led it to be compared to a *custom-made suit*. Another important aspect emphasised is the enhanced respect for the individual's voice and preferences.

> I think the design and spirit [of the law] are much better, much more innovative, much more respectful. (B4, Medical Expert)

This was often illustrated by the inclusion in the new law of provisions, such as the mandatory direct hearing of the beneficiary.

Recent and Demanding Legislation

While the positive aspects are acknowledged, there is also broad awareness that adopting and internalising a novel legal framework is a challenging process, especially when it requires a substantial shift in perspectives and professional practices. In this regard, both judicial system actors and representatives from the disability service provision sector have noted that they are still working to refine and improve procedures to better align with the spirit of the new law.

Inconsistencies in the Interpretation and Application of the Law

Discrepancies have been noted in the interpretation and application of specific legal provisions, especially regarding the mandate to directly hear the beneficiaries. In seeking to adapt this requirement to each case, taking into account available resources as well as the interpretations and preferences of different judicial officers, highly varied practices have emerged.

This variation has raised concerns about how this right to be heard is ensured, particularly in terms of maintaining equitable conditions for all beneficiaries.

> There are various interpretations, particularly regarding this issue of the direct hearings. Some courts require the person to appear in court. Others, if the person cannot come, send representatives to their location. Or, in some cases, a forensic report is requested without conducting it on-site or without the presence of magistrates. (C6 Public Prosecutor)

Resource Shortages

A key challenge reported to fully implement the framework set by the CRPD is the lack of resources in the courts, a problem further intensified by the high volume of cases. It was pointed out that the new law classifies all Accompanied Adult Regime cases as urgent, without considering the already heavy workload of the courts and without allocating additional human or technical resources to manage these requests. This shortfall creates tensions and inconsistencies, ultimately undermining the intended goal of tailoring support decisions to an individual's needs through a thorough and careful assessment. As one magistrate noted:

> We [Public Prosecutor's Office] do not have the human resources to handle so many requests. (…) Of course, if I processed all the cases the same way I used to handle interdiction proceedings, I could clear 100 cases in no time and keep my workload under control. However, I cannot treat the Accompanied Adult Regime cases the same way as the former guardianship regime, because that is not the intended approach, nor does it align with the philosophy behind the new law. (C5 Public Prosecutor)

These challenges are also closely linked to New Public Management models (Hood, 1991) being applied to the judicial system that continues to prioritise efficiency over adequacy and quality, creating tensions in the roles of magistrates and forensic experts:

> This new law clashes with the pressure to do everything faster, faster, and faster… because this law is inherently slower! What I see is the difficulty of

> reconciling the careful approach the law requires with the urgency it also demands. (B4 Expert)

Misinterpretation of Directives and Unjustified Requirements

Interviewees also highlighted challenges extending beyond the judicial sphere that influence the appropriate use and implementation of the Accompanied Adult Regime. A key concern is the misinterpretation of directives by some public servants, leading to the imposition of unjustified requirements and, consequently, an increase in requests for formal support measures under the law.

> They all come here with instructions from Social Security [that] to receive a certain pension, they must have Accompanied Adult registered on the birth certificate. Wrong, it has nothing to do with it, does it? (C6 Public Prosecutor)

Challenges in the Identification of Adequate Supporters

Several interviewees also reported that there were instances where it was difficult to identify suitable and available individuals to appoint as supporters, due to the limited or non-existent social network of many persons with disabilities, outside the service provider they attend. The challenges involved in managing these processes were extensively discussed by the interviewees, with some suggesting the possibility of creating a pool of professionals to ensure support to these beneficiaries.

Inadequacy and/or Insufficiency of Support Services in the Community

Another aspect highlighted was the inadequacy of the current typologies of social services. It was suggested that there is a need to rethink these services in light of a person-centred approach, which would provide a more adequate response to individuals' different support needs. In some cases, this could mean dispensing or complementing, in a more effective way, the formal support offered within the scope of the Accompanied Adult Regime.

With respect to community-based support responses, beyond the ethical tensions arising from the dual role of professionals as both service providers and accompanying persons, the significant pressure on most service providers further complicates their ability to take on additional responsibilities:

> Imagine the challenge of running an institution without sufficient backup support and having to find accompanying persons. This is tough because if you have 50 clients, you need someone to be a tutor or accompanying person for 4, 5, 6, 7, or even 8 clients. This often leads to a generic approach to support, rather than individualised care. (A2 President of the Board of Directors of a disability service-provider organisation)

Training Gaps and the Persistence of a Paternalistic and Medical Model of Disability

A problem that has been identified upstream of the legislation itself is the persistence of paternalistic and medical views on disability. This hinders the alignment of conceptualisations and practices with the assumptions of the human rights model enshrined in the CRPD:

> Mentalities take time to change, don't they? Mentalities are not changed with decree-laws, nor with laws. For example, and I can speak at the level of the judiciary, I see that there are colleagues who still look at the new Regime as if it were the same thing as Guardianship (*Interdição*), only the name has changed. (C5 Public Prosecutor)

In this regard, gaps in human rights training were also highlighted, namely in some curricula of initial law training, which do not include in-depth content on human rights, much less on the rights of persons with disabilities, and the notion of legal capacity and equal recognition before the law advanced by Article 12 of the CRPD.

Focus Groups with Persons with Intellectual and Psychosocial Disabilities

Four focus groups involving individuals with psychosocial or intellectual disabilities who had been subject to guardianship or Accompanied Adult Regime measures (*N* = 19) were co-conducted by the research team with four non-academic researchers with disabilities. The focus groups enabled us to gather firsthand accounts of lived experiences regarding the exercise or limitation of rights. They used participatory methodologies, such as Self-Determination Maps and Rivers of Life (Pinto et al., 2024), which served as starting points for group discussions about individual experiences and perceptions of rights. After carrying out the above activities, the non-academic researchers presented the participants with two photos that they had taken and selected for this purpose: one about 'my choices' and the other about 'barriers to my choices'. Based on the photos, the participants discussed the barriers to their choices, what people with disabilities can't do and the situations in which they have autonomy and decision-making power. The focus groups were fully transcribed. Thematic analysis was undertaken (Braun et al., 2019), with the participation of the non-academic researchers, to provide an in-depth understanding of the data.

Lives Entangled in Relations of Inequality and Power

In addition to court ruling restricting rights beyond what would be expected or reasonable, limits to self-determination are also imposed on the everyday lives of persons with intellectual and psychosocial disabilities. In some cases, the continued repetition of this pattern of interaction leads to the internalisation, by the people themselves, of negative self-representations, thus contributing to their disempowerment. Testimonies such as those collected in one of the focus groups (FG4) attest to this:

Facilitator: In your day-to-day life, can you do whatever you want?
Participant 3: No, we must do what we are told.
Participant 1: I have to ask, "Can I go to the party, or will you let me go to the party?". And they say "yes" or "no". If they say "yes", I'll go. If they say no, "look, you'll go later with your sister". And I do that.

Disempowerment and Dependency

Restrictions on rights and the imposition of substitute decision-making, in contrast to the support mechanisms envisioned by the CRPD, are often justified by a perceived need to protect individuals deemed vulnerable due to cognitive or mental health conditions. However, many participants of the focus groups reported how they actively contribute to their communities, notably through engagement in the so-called socially useful activities, undertaking demanding tasks two to four days a week. Despite their efforts, these roles remain severely undervalued, with earnings typically falling below €100 per month. The following exchange from a focus group (FG3) illustrates not only the financial precarity experienced by participants but also the power dynamics governing the management of their financial resources:

Participant 1: Not long ago my mother passed away. They didn't let me see my mother and abandoned me. I haven't seen them for seven years. (…) I'm being controlled, the money I earn, she's the one who manages the accounts. She only gives me a certain amount per week.
Participant 4: Is she good to you?
Participant 1: (…) I have a certain resentment about the Accompanied Adult, because I think that the money that my aunt gives me is little. 20€ per week, it's nothing!

This testimony underscores the ongoing disempowerment faced by many individuals under restrictive support arrangements. The management of financial assets, often dictated by third parties, exemplifies broader patterns of control that limit autonomy and reinforce dependency, ultimately sidelining the voices of those directly affected.

Awareness of Rights and Capabilities

Although the marginalisation of the voices and will of individuals with intellectual and psychosocial disabilities remains prevalent, the focus groups also highlighted a growing awareness of their citizenship rights and capabilities. Participants expressed frustration and resistance to unwarranted limitations on their rights and autonomy, signalling a shift toward greater self-advocacy and empowerment:

> Our rights, one of them is the fight against stigma. Because society creates a lot of stigma: "Look, that guy over there is crazy. He's crazy, he's no good for anything." We get angry about that. We're not crazy, we're not sick, we're people, men and women with our rights… that's it." (EC 6)

Conclusion

The findings from the EQUAL project presented above underline the recognition that the Accompanied Adults Act represents a significant legislative advance, more closely aligned with a human rights-based approach to disability. Judicial decisions regarding accompanying measures have gradually become less restrictive, reflecting a shift towards greater respect for individual autonomy. However, most of the court rulings still prioritise narratives of vulnerability, dependence and protection, resulting in an overrepresentation of decisions that impose general representation or severely restrict personal rights.

The full integration of the human rights model advanced by the CRPD and the Accompanied Adult Law remains a complex challenge. Continued reliance on the medical model, which often shapes medical assessments influencing court decisions, emphasises incapacity rather than promotes a comprehensive assessment of needs and abilities. Such an understanding of disability, as a medical, vulnerable and irrational condition requiring protection, as well as containment and control (Foucault, 1976), is signalled by the substantial proportion of judicial decisions that remove personal rights, particularly those concerned with financial and reproductive rights.

Beyond the judicial system, structural barriers hinder the effective and consistent application of the law. The judiciary's shortage of technical and human resources, coupled with insufficient community-based support services, and some misinterpretation of directives, limits the capacity to implement individually tailored and rights-based support measures. There is also a recognition of current gaps in the training of judicial actors, who lack a view of disability anchored in the human rights model (Lawson & Beckett, 2021). All of these barriers suggest that the implementation of the new Accompanied Adult Regime has been captured (Krieger, 2003) by numerous social, political and economic forces that reduce its impact and effectiveness in promoting substantive change, even though it can be seen as a transformative law that underpins a paradigm shift in the recognition of the legal capacity of persons with disabilities in Portugal. Not surprisingly, the life histories of many persons with disability continue to be marked by relations of inequality and, in some situations, the internalisation and reproduction of negative self-representations, particularly those that associate disability with dependency. Despite these reported challenges, focus group participants with intellectual and psychosocial disabilities expressed a growing awareness of their rights, affecting their attitudes and their fight for self-determination, legal capacity and personal autonomy. This evolving awareness may signal an important cultural and institutional shift, underscoring the need for continued efforts to ensure that legal frameworks and support systems fully realise the principles of autonomy, inclusion and dignity enshrined in the CRPD.

References

Braun, V., Clarke, V., Hayfield, N., & Terry, G. (2019). Thematic Analysis. In *Handbook of Research Methods in Health Social Sciences* (pp. 843–860). Springer. https://doi.org/10.1007/978-981-10-5251-4_103

Foucault, M. (1976). *Histoire de la Folie à l'Âge Classique*. Gallimard.

Frezzo, M. (2015). *The Sociology of Human Rights*. Polity Press.

Hood, C. (1991). A Public Management for All Seasons? *Public Administration, 69*(1), 3–19. https://doi.org/10.1111/J.1467-9299.1991.TB00779.X

Krieger, L. H. (2003). Sociolegal Backlash. In L. H. Krieger (Ed.), *Backlash Against the ADA: Reinterpreting Disability Rights* (pp. 340–393). The University of Michigan Press.

Lawson, A., & Beckett, A. E. (2021). The Social and Human Rights Models of Disability: Towards a Complementarity Thesis. *The International Journal of Human Rights, 25*(2), 348–379.

Pinto, P. C. (2023). Disability and Human Rights. In R. L. Brown, M. Maroto, & D. Pettinicchio (Eds.), *The Oxford Handbook of the Sociology of Human Rights* (pp. 175–194). Oxford University Press.

Pinto, P. C., Pinto, T. J., Neca, P., & Maltez, B. (2024). *Doing Inclusive Research Guided by Human Rights Principles with Persons with Intellectual and Psychosocial Disabilities: Potential and Challenges* (Sage Research Methods: Diversifying and Decolonizing Research). SAGE Publications Ltd. https://doi.org/10.4135/9781529691160

Open Access This chapter is licensed under the terms of the Creative Commons Attribution 4.0 International License (http://creativecommons.org/licenses/by/4.0/), which permits use, sharing, adaptation, distribution and reproduction in any medium or format, as long as you give appropriate credit to the original author(s) and the source, provide a link to the Creative Commons license and indicate if changes were made.

The images or other third party material in this chapter are included in the chapter's Creative Commons license, unless indicated otherwise in a credit line to the material. If material is not included in the chapter's Creative Commons license and your intended use is not permitted by statutory regulation or exceeds the permitted use, you will need to obtain permission directly from the copyright holder.

Part II

"In our own words": Legal Capacity Through Life Stories

Disability and legal capacity are social constructs created and negotiated at different times and in different settings. As signalled in Part I, disabled people's legal capacity and legal agency have been greatly influenced by normative and disabling ideas of the body, of mental capacity, and of decision-making capacity. People with cognitive, sensory and psychosocial impairments have been particularly affected by these ideas and values. The adoption of the UN CRPD in 2006 paved the way for a paradigmatic social, cultural and legal transformation in this area. In Portugal, these changes only materialized after 2018, with the publication of the new regime of the Accompanied Adult (Law 49/2018). Social, cultural and legal changes are, however, distinct dimensions when analysing the impact of the inaugurated regime on disabled people's lives. Part II is thus devoted to people's life stories, where formal legal rules, social and cultural norms and values condense, framing disabled people's lives. These lives are, therefore, pivotal to analysing any real-life policy change.

The following life stories of *Oscar, Samuel, Sophie, Mary, John and Peter* are not representative of the group of people particularly affected by this legal change in Portugal but are meant to represent the main barriers faced in its implementation. These names are not real for anonymity reasons, and other names of people, places and/or institutions mentioned have been eliminated and/or changed to protect people's identities. These six narratives have been constructed through disabled people's voices, collected in semi-structured interviews, but also with the support, whenever possible and available, of court decisions and other documents of the legal proceedings, namely medical and forensic assessments. Since we wanted to create a space to listen to voices that are too often silenced and denied, we deliberately chose not to author these chapters but to name them after their protagonists.

Yet, these life stories do not aspire to narrate the entire lives of the people portrayed; rather, they aim to capture the essence of what has happened in their lives, their experiences and feelings regarding self-determination and the impact of this policy.

The six chapters in this Part II thus allow a better analysis of the past and present reality of disabled people's experiences of rights, particularly the right to legal capacity, the diversity of factors affecting legal reform and the impact of formal and informal restrictions of rights on disabled people's everyday life. Furthermore, they help us identify the threads that frame the legal capacity reform in Portugal, and perhaps even beyond, in light of twenty-first-century human rights. But to this we will return in the concluding chapter.

5

Oscar's Story: "I just want my life back"

Paula Campos Pinto

Abstract Oscar's story recounts his disrupted childhood, institutionalisation, and loss of legal capacity. He was raised in foster care and later in an institution, where he managed to build supportive relationships. As an adult, he worked at a recycling company and moved around by himself in the community on his motorcycle. However, when the Social Security Administration required all social benefits recipients to have a bank account in order to continue receiving disability benefits, the court imposed guardianship, thereby removing Oscar's legal capacity and seven other personal rights, including the right to freedom of movement. With support and preparation, he appealed, and in Fall 2024, he regained mobility, although financial management remained supervised. Job loss

Interview conducted and analysed by Paula Campos Pinto.

P. Campos Pinto (✉)
Observatory on Disability and Human Rights and Interdisciplinary Centre on Gender Studies, Institute of Social and Political Sciences, University of Lisbon, Lisbon, Portugal
e-mail: mppinto@edu.ulisboa.pt

© The Author(s) 2026

P. Campos Pinto et al. (eds.), *Equal Rights, Equal Voices*, Palgrave Socio-Legal Studies,
https://doi.org/10.1007/978-3-032-05969-7_5

and personal setbacks followed, highlighting the intersectional inequalities and structural ableism that compounded Oscar's life.

Keywords Capacity contract • Guardianship • Intersectional inequalities • Structural ableism

Oscar was born in one of the largest cities in the country, in 1985, following an unplanned pregnancy. Shortly after his birth, the couple split; his father started a new relationship with the younger sister of Oscar's mother, who, as a result, developed a profound depression. His father and grandfather took care of Oscar. From these early days, which he nevertheless recalls as "happy times", he remembers playing football with his dad. Little more is known or said about his childhood. At an unknown age and for unspoken reasons, Oscar was placed into foster care 300 km away from his biological family. It is in this new city that he started primary school.

He lived with the foster care family and three other children for close to a decade, but he does not recall much about those years. In 1999, when he was fourteen years old, one of the children under the care of the foster family died. Faced with some "other problems" that Oscar did not want to disclose, the foster mother fell ill and became unable to continue caring for Oscar and the children—and so he had to move again. This time, he was admitted to a large institution for children and youngsters at risk located in the central region of the country. The following years were marked by the friendship developed with one male staff of that institution—Oscar described how he was often invited to spend Christmas day and Easter with this young man's family, and even to celebrate with them his own birthday: "I call him my brother. I call his father, Dad, and his mother, Mom. His sister is my sister. They are my second family", Oscar confided, suggesting that despite being institutionalised, he could count, at least episodically, on close and affectionate relationships around him throughout his adolescence years. His biological father would also visit from time to time, or Oscar would take the train and pay him a visit. Yet, it is also during his teenage years that Oscar started exhibiting aggressive, difficult behaviour. At the age of fourteen, Oscar was still attending grade four.[1]

In July 2001, Oscar left school and initiated a training course in gardening in a nearby vocational training centre for persons with intellectual disabilities.[2] One year later, he moved back with his mother, stepfather, and young half-brother, who by then were living one hour away from the vocational school he attended, in a small town near the coast. Yet the travel distance to the training centre, and the "lack of time and money of the family" forced him to quit the programme just one year later, in July 2002, without completing the training. To this date, Oscar keeps friendships from those days, with whom he continues to call or exchange through Facebook.

A few months later, in March 2003, Oscar enrolled in another training centre facility for persons with intellectual disabilities, this one closer to home, where he again started a vocational training programme in gardening. The new centre was located on a very large estate of about 140 hectares that used to be a former health facility. Although the legacy of the place's history is endowed with beautiful trees and is located close to the beach, the property is fenced and separated from the surrounding community by a gate that only authorised people and vehicles are allowed to cross in and out.

Oscar was one of those who entered and left the place every day, as he continued to live in the nearby village with his mother and stepfamily. However, three months into the programme, the stepfather requested that Oscar be placed in residential care, another service provided by the same service provider and also located on the premises. So, Oscar moved

[1] In the Portuguese educational system, children attending grade four are typically nine years old.

[2] Funded by the European Social Fund and the Portuguese government, vocational training programmes for persons with disabilities in Portugal are typically more extended in hours than regular vocational training to address specific learning needs of this group. Through a combination of social policy measures and supports, they aim to develop technical and social skills to promote the inclusion of trainees in the labour market, but their success rate in promoting the transition to the labour market is limited. Often, trainees rotate among centres after finishing a course, as they are not allowed to do more than one course in each centre—attending a training programme becomes their main occupation, which also has helped foster a vocational training "industry" (Albrecht, 1992) in the country.

to the group home facility there. This move would have larger implications in Oscar's life, though.

First, due to the funding rules in place at the time, Oscar was no longer allowed to attend the training programme when placed in residential care. Therefore, for the second time, Oscar had to quit the training. While he remained in the same organisation and geographic location, he had to be enrolled in the then called *Occupational Activities Centre* (CAO), a day care centre for people deemed "unable to work" that provided activities as well as social and therapeutic support. Attendees of CAOs can develop "socially useful activities", preferably in the open labour market, but they cannot receive a salary for the work done, just a small stipend. Nor are they entitled to any social benefits. To this date, Oscar is still living in the residential care and remains a client of the now designated *Centre of Activities and Capacitation for Inclusion* (CACI) of this organisation, whose norms do not differ much from those applied before in CAOs.

The CAO (later CACI) offered several workshops, and Oscar liked being busy and doing manual work. So, he started learning how to make roasters out of recycled parts; he made a small compressor, then he started doing recycling work, taking electric and electronic devices apart (washing machines, computers, plasmas, old televisions). He removed the parts and then separated them into components that were sold to a company that would come every month or so to pick them up.

Oscar was very meticulous and focused on his work. Sometimes, he would also make small repairs. He enjoyed the work and did such a good job that he won the right to a special desk and toolbox in a designated corner of the workshop. Every day, he went in, put on his headphones, and did his work. He was happy with his life.

Around 2010, he also started attending karate classes in the community. He got along very well with his master, quickly progressing through the ranks, from White to Yellow, then Orange, Brown, up to Black Belt. He was so good at it that the master invited him to teach the young kids. Yet, humble, Oscar refused:

> I never gave training sessions; the master called me to, but I didn't want to train the little ones. I didn't think I knew how to give the training to the little ones properly. My colleagues, Isabel and Johny, and others, they

started training the little ones; they have the Katas better trained than I do. I didn't, but I reached my goal, I got my black belt.

In the organisation where he continued to live and work, Oscar thrived. He started a loving relationship with another client of the CAO. Her grandfather grew fond of him and promised to offer him a motorcycle if he learned to bike on two wheels. And in just one week, with the help of a staff member at the CAO, Oscar did learn. So, he received a motorcycle as a gift. On weekends, Oscar would drive his motorcycle to visit his girlfriend and spend time with her family. Every morning, he would call her to make sure she got up in time to pick up the bus and come to the daycare centre she also attended.

In the workshop, when there was no recycling work to do, Oscar helped with whatever work was available. Lately, the organisation is building dog kennels, large and small, to be sold in a pet shop in the community. He also joined all kinds of social activities organised by the centre, such as indoor parties, trips to the beach or swimming pool, and movie nights in the nearby city. On his motorcycle, Oscar would also often drive to the local community on his own, just to walk around the local fair, buy his "little things", meet friends or go to karate classes. He felt free and in control. "I lived my normal life" as he described it. Between work and socialisation, in and outside the walls of the institution, life went on as usual. Driving around the local community, Oscar never got lost, never got into trouble, never had an accident. If he had to travel far, someone would give him a lift, or he would take a taxi. Everyone liked him.

Given his status as a CAO client, Oscar was a recipient of a disability benefit. Every month, he would get in the mail his Social Security check, which he would then take to a bank to cash. In 2018, however, Social Security suddenly changed the rules: instead of sending out checks, it announced that wire transfers would be made to send money directly into recipients' bank accounts. The problem was that Oscar, like many other people with intellectual disabilities, did not have a bank account because no bank would open an account for a person with intellectual disabilities. To obtain a bank account in his name, Oscar needed a guardian to sign for him and take responsibility for managing his financial affairs. As Oscar's natural family continued to be absent from his life, it was the service provider that Oscar was attending that presented the legal claim for Oscar's guardianship.

A few months later, Oscar was summed to court. It was an awful experience. Oscar went in with the director of the association that he attended (who later became his accompanying person) and the coordinator of the residential care facility. They sat in the back and Oscar in the front:

> And they, the doctor and then the judge, started asking questions, they started bombarding me with everything in a row, they didn't even give me time to think before I answered. They asked me for a 50 euro note, for some clothes, how much I'd get in change. They started bombarding me, several things, several things in a row. They didn't give me time to think, they didn't give me time to answer. And I blocked it. I couldn't say anything more.

The decision came soon after, and Oscar's world was turned upside down. Although the new Accompanied Adult Scheme was already in place, allowing for a flexible approach to support based on individual needs, the judge ruled on a substitute decision-making model and imposed a severe restriction on Oscar's rights, including depriving him of seven personal rights. Among them, she removed Oscar's liberty of movement so he was no longer allowed to travel by himself outside the walls of the institution. He could no longer take his motorcycle to visit his girlfriend at home, to meet friends in the village or to attend karate classes. He felt sad, diminished, hurt. He could not understand why this was being done to him. The staff at the association was also astonished by the decision, so together with Oscar, they decided to enter an appeal. This time, Oscar would have to be ready—at the Centre, Oscar started practicing the answers to the questions that he could be asked in the court.

In the meantime, the Centre was able to find a recycling company that was willing to take in Oscar for a few days a week in exchange for a modest stipend. In the Fall 2023, Oscar started working in this company twice a week, separating the components of electronic devices. It was hard work, 8-hours standing at the counter, in a hot warehouse, wearing steel toe boots, gloves, and protective glasses all day to be safe at work.

But Oscar greatly enjoyed it and made new friends—on his birthday, he even bought a cake and shared it with his coworkers. His boss gave him a refurbished tablet as a birthday gift.

Since he could no longer travel by himself, to get to work, Oscar had to get up very early and take the bus of the association. The bus left the premises every morning at 7am to pick up some clients and bring them back to CACI for daily activities. Because the bus went around the community for several pickups, it would take Oscar an hour to get to work. At the end of the day, the same thing—sometimes Oscar had to wait an hour or so for the bus to come around and bring him back to the centre. Still, he was happy to be able to do work outside the association. He felt that his boss liked him and respected his work. With the little money he could save, he was able to buy a new mountain bicycle to run around the estate.

In the association, when he does not go outside for work, Oscar also follows a pretty established routine—every morning he gets up, takes his medication and fixes his breakfast. In the group home where he lives, the residents cook their own meals and do the housework. After breakfast, Oscar walks to the workshop for work. Lunch takes place in the main cafeteria with the other clients and staff of the CACI. After lunch, he meets his girlfriend and a group of friends for coffee at one of the facilities owned by the association on the estate. Then he goes back to his counter at the workshop. At the end of the day, Oscar returns home. He takes a quick shower, makes dinner and eats with the other residents. He washes the dishes, does the laundry and takes care of his female dog—she is very old now, almost blind, and has trouble walking due to a heart attack she had a few years ago. Oscar must feed her, give her medication and take her for walks on a leash. When freed from all his duties, he enjoys watching TV or just lying in his bed while listening to music, talking on the phone, or surfing the Internet.

Sometimes, friends and staff give Oscar old devices that no longer work. Instead of separating the parts, Oscar, with the help of his monitor, tries to repair them. When he is able to do so, he is allowed to keep them to take home—he managed to fix a coffee machine that now stands in the kitchen at the group home, and also a toaster that only had a broken wire. He likes to keep busy and feels very proud of these achievements.

Nevertheless, Oscar does not envision himself living outside the institution, getting married, or having children. Perhaps this desire may arise in the future, but not for now, he says. For now, he feels welcomed and cared for in the association, and he is quite happy with the relationships he has built with the staff, other clients, and his girlfriend. Spending weekends at her house and seeing her every day at the association is quite enough for him, even though, following the court decision, he can no longer leave the premises without the president's permission (who is also his Support Person) and always has to be accompanied by someone. For lack of staff, sometimes there is no one available to go out with Oscar when he wants, but he understands those constraints and accepts them quietly. He is longing to have his sentence revised, though, to regain his freedom of movement.

Every money that Oscar earns, either at the CACI or at the recycling company, goes to his bank account. It is from this account (where Oscar also receives his disability pension) that all his living expenses are paid: the tuition of the CACI, Oscar's medication, clothes, and meals. However, Oscar does not possess a credit or debit card. Every month, a staff member from the association sends to his Accompanying Person (who is also the president of the association) the list of Oscar's monthly expenses and she makes the payments. When Oscar needs or wants to buy something extra, he must discuss the issue with her. He just keeps with him pocket money to buy his daily coffee and a little more. More recently, Oscar requested that the money he makes at the company be kept in the association instead of in the bank. This makes things more expeditious when he needs to buy something for himself. The supporter agreed, so the association now keeps a book where the money that Oscar brings in or withdraws is noted down.

Sometimes, there is not enough money for the things that Oscar wants to buy—so a staff member explains him why and he understands that he needs to save for a little longer. That is how he bought his mountain bike.

Oscar is not interested in politics, so being able to exercise his right to vote is not something he really cares about. He does not trust politicians, except the President of the Republic, who once visited the association. Oscar and some colleagues were invited to meet him, and they sat at the same table. He found him a wonderful person and would certainly vote for him if he stood up for election again.

In general, Oscar gets along well with everyone, and everyone likes him. One day, at the workshop, though, a new CACI client insulted and offended one of his friends. He even became violent—picking up a tool, he was about to hit him. Oscar stood between the two of them and stopped him. He then complained to the director of the centre. He finds this new client quite rude.

Oscar had no recollection of being discriminated against because of his disability: on the contrary, he felt that his fellow karate practitioners, people in the community, and at work treat him fairly and as an equal to everyone else. He never had any reason to complain, except now, in relation to the court ruling. That is something he cannot accept—he feels discriminated against, he wants to be able to move around freely as he used to do, to go to the beach and play football with his friends. He wants his life back. So, he hopes to be able to go before the judge again soon to reverse the decision. Then, maybe one day, he will be able to get a real job, own a place and move in with his girlfriend. Who knows? Maybe one day…

The Court Decision

Oscar's judicial process started in 2018, following a Social Security demand to open a bank account, something he could not do since banks in Portugal refuse to open accounts to persons with intellectual impairments. On behalf of Oscar, the non-profit organisation where he lived initiated the case through the public prosecutor's office. The court appointed a lawyer to argue the case on Oscar's defence, but the lawyer never got in touch with him, and she did not oppose the claim.

Following one session in court, with Oscar, the lawyer, a medical expert and the judge, a sentence was issued in September 2019. In it, to ground his decision, the judge starts by providing a medical description that portrays Oscar as "a person with a moderate intellectual impairment, presenting behavioural changes and epilepsy (G40 of ICD-10)". Drawing from the medical reports collected, the judge further affirms that Oscar has had "a history of recurrent reactive depressions (…) with characteristics of resistance to antidepressant therapy and tranquilizers, (…) bouts of heteroaggressiveness that are difficult to control (…), showing signs of intellectual and behavioral deterioration, translated by the inability to adapt to any training or activity that is assigned to him". As such, he concludes, Oscar requires "supervision for meals cooking, hygiene and medication (…) and permanent support from the institution". In short, the judge is poised that Oscar has "an irreversible condition which presents from birth", and that none of these facts are questionable or need further proof.

In the second part of the sentence, the judge develops the legal arguments for the decision issued. Citing Article 138 of the Portuguese Civil Code, which introduces the Accompanied Adult Scheme, she deems that the two conditions alluded to in this norm are verified in Oscar's case: first, the "repeated impossibility of self-determination regarding duties and rights" and second, the fact that this impossibility derives from a health condition. While recalling that the Accompanied Adult Scheme aims to ensure "the well-being, recovery and full exercise of rights and duties", she reminds that the range of support measures that can be determined in no case "should deprive the individual of his personal rights nor of carrying out everyday business, unless the sentence itself so determines". Nonetheless, she carries on, the "proven facts (….) impose the conclusion that the defendant, for reasons of disability, is permanently incapable of self-determination regarding the fulfillment of his duties or the exercise of his personal and property rights". Hence, she concludes, "the gravity of his condition (…) justify and impose the appointment of someone to manage his assets and take all necessary decisions for his well-being - present and future".

It is in the third part of the sentence that the detail of the judicial decision is laid down. The judge orders the measure of "general representation" and the "deprivation of carrying out everyday business" and specifically withdraws seven personal rights: the right to marry, the right to procreate, the right to parenting or adopt, the right to choose a profession, the right to move around in the country or abroad, the right to decide where to live, the right to write a testament. The judge appoints as support person the president of the association that Oscar attends.

Epilogue

After learning about the sentence that so drastically changed his life, Oscar, with the assistance of the association's president and staff, initiated a long process to reverse the decision. Unlike the previous status of interdiction, which was determined once for life, the Accompanied Adult Scheme must be revised every five years. The staff at the association started teaching Oscar about the value of money and trained him to be more assertive when presenting himself again before the court.

In Spring 2024, Oscar was summoned to the court again. Once again, a lawyer was appointed to defend him. And again, the lawyer did not get in touch with Oscar to learn about his needs, abilities and interests. They saw each other in the waiting room outside the court for the first time, but not even then were there any exchange between the two. Oscar only found out that he was his lawyer inside the court room when the judge called on him for the initial statement. Not surprisingly, he had nothing to add or say.

Yet this time Oscar was ready. He answered all the questions and stood up to defend his rights, especially the right to move around freely. The association also provided updated reports demonstrating Oscar multiple abilities and life skills.

In fall 2024, the decision came out—Oscar regained his freedom. He felt exhilarated; he could again drive his motorbike in the community, as the new legal decision only provided for accompanying measures regarding the management of his financial affairs.

As he was still celebrating this victory and enjoying his regained freedom, life faced a new turn—on New Year's Day, the director of the CACI programme that Oscar attended received an email from the recycling company where he worked twice a week. The company had not paid Oscar's stipend for the last few months, but in this email, the company was breaking down the agreement and dismissing Oscar for good. The company was running into financial difficulties—Oscar had to go.

It was a hard hit for Oscar—he misses his work colleagues with whom he had become friends, and above all, he misses going outside the walls of the institution regularly and the feeling of purpose and value that he had gotten from work. By then, he had also broken up with his girlfriend and quitted karate classes because the old master no longer trains there, and he does not get along so well with the new one. So, once again, Oscar's world shrunk and lost some of its colours. Yet Oscar is not breaking. Drawing from old friendships in the community, he is helping a friend at the local market to make some money and keep busy while waiting for the staff at the association to find a new recycling company that is willing to take him in. The fight has started all over again.

Comment

Oscar's story is a powerful illustration of the legacy of the *capacity contract* (Clifford, 2014; Simplican, 2015), which bases entitlement to full citizenship on a threshold level of mental capacity. Although legal reform in Portugal, with the introduction of the Accompanied Adult framework, enables more tailored arrangements of supports, the court ruled a severe restriction of Oscar's rights and liberty of movement, *de facto* imposing a guardianship or substitute decision-making regime that violates the provisions of Article 12 of the Convention on the Rights of Persons with Disabilities (CRPD) and the content of General Comment N°. 1 of the CRPD Committee. In the old-fashioned way, the judge equated mental capacity (the ability to understand certain facts or concepts) with legal capacity (the ability to make decisions that are recognised by the law), as if they were one and the same thing. From a human rights perspective, they are not—but for Oscar (and other persons with intellectual disability) to enjoy full legal capacity, it is necessary more than just legal reform: it requires attitudinal change to enable a focus on individual capacities rather than on impairments, and the provision of adequate supports and accommodations to assist with decision-making (Flynn & Arstein-Kerslake, 2014). This also means moving from the idea of protection to that of recognition and respect for the dignity of a full citizen (Glen, 2015). People under guardianship regimes may indeed face increased vulnerability, as the total power the law gives to guardians may exacerbate opportunities for abuse (Arstein-Kerslake, 2016).

It is not Oscar's case, although the fact that his support person is also the president of the association where he lives creates an undeniable conflict of interest.

Faced with a harsh sentence that he could neither understand nor accept, Oscar fought to get his "life back", eventually succeeding. Yet despite this important victory, he is enduring hardships again.

Viewed through a long-range lens, Oscar's life trajectory is shaped by layers of intersectional inequalities: a disrupted family, a history of foster care and institutionalisation, economic insecurity, limited opportunities to pursue work and the constant disruption of emotional bonds. All of these are inevitably intertwined with structural ableism—"a system of historical and contemporary policies, institutions, societal norms, and practices that devalue and disadvantage people who are disabled" (Lundberg & Chen, 2023, p. 1). Despite legal reform, these multiple intersecting systems of oppression continue to compound the social exclusion, economic exploitation and marginalisation of so many persons with intellectual disabilities who, like Oscar, are deprived of their full citizenship and rights.

References

Albrecht, G. L. (1992). *The Disability Business: Rehabilitation in America*. SAGE Publications.

Arstein-Kerslake, A. (2016). An Empowering Dependency: Exploring Support for the Exercise of Legal Capacity. *Scandinavian Journal of Disability Research, 18*(1), 77–92. https://doi.org/10.1080/15017419.2014.941926

Clifford, S. (2014). Politics, Groups, and Identities the Capacity Contract: Locke, Disability, and the Political Exclusion of "Idiots". *Politics, Groups, and Identities, 2*, 90–103. https://doi.org/10.1080/21565503.2013.876918

Flynn, E., & Arstein-Kerslake, A. (2014). Legislating Personhood: Realising the Right to Support in Exercising Legal Capacity. *International Journal of Law in Context, 10*(1), 81–104. https://doi.org/10.1017/S1744552313000384

Glen, K. B. (2015). Supported Decision-Making and the Human Right of Legal Capacity. *INCLUSION, 3*(1), 2–16. https://doi.org/10.1352/2326-6988-3.1.2

Lundberg, D. J., & Chen, J. A. (2023). Structural Ableism in Public Health and Healthcare: A Definition and Conceptual Framework. *The Lancet Regional Health - Americas, 30*(100650), 1–8. https://doi.org/10.1016/J.LANA.2023.100650

Simplican, S. C. (2015). *The Capacity Contract: Intellectual Disability and the Question of Citizenship*. University of Minnesota Press.

Open Access This chapter is licensed under the terms of the Creative Commons Attribution 4.0 International License (http://creativecommons.org/licenses/by/4.0/), which permits use, sharing, adaptation, distribution and reproduction in any medium or format, as long as you give appropriate credit to the original author(s) and the source, provide a link to the Creative Commons license and indicate if changes were made.

The images or other third party material in this chapter are included in the chapter's Creative Commons license, unless indicated otherwise in a credit line to the material. If material is not included in the chapter's Creative Commons license and your intended use is not permitted by statutory regulation or exceeds the permitted use, you will need to obtain permission directly from the copyright holder.

6

Mary's Story—"What's in a court decision": The Construction of Disabled People's Legal (In)capacity

Fernando Fontes

Abstract Mary, a 40-year-old mother of two, experienced psychiatric diagnoses and mild cognitive impairment. Her family initiated guardianship proceedings in 2013 to resolve debts; forensic assessments and medical reports described cognitive deficits and inability to manage affairs. In 2015, the court imposed guardianship, appointing her parents and transferring parental responsibility for her daughter to her sister. Mary was often unheard in proceedings, confused about assessments and fearful of hospitalization or of losing her children. Despite legal reforms, her daily life remained controlled: medication, routines, and supervised work. Mary's case illustrates medical dominance, procedural injustice, and the persistence of restrictive regimes that still affect so many persons with intellectual and psychosocial disabilities.

Interview conducted and analysed by Fernando Fontes.

F. Fontes (✉)
Centro de Estudos Sociais, University of Coimbra, Coimbra, Portugal
e-mail: fernandofontes@ces.uc.pt

© The Author(s) 2026

P. Campos Pinto et al. (eds.), *Equal Rights, Equal Voices*, Palgrave Socio-Legal Studies,
https://doi.org/10.1007/978-3-032-05969-7_6

Keywords Guardianship • Capture of the law • Psychosocial disabilities • Sexual and reproductive rights

The Context

Mary is a 40-year-old woman, mother of two children: a 15-year-old boy and a 13-year-old girl. Mary has had several diagnoses across her life: persistent depressive disorder, generalized anxiety disorder, neurotic depression and mild cognitive impairment. Mary is a very quiet person with a friendly smile that seems to conceal an inner struggle between what people want her to do and be and her willing. This inner struggle emerges in the tears that burst when speaking about her life and about her children during the interview and in the repeated idea that "at the time, she was not in the right headspace!". This appeaser is pronounced in a naturalized way, denoting its inner and outer reiteration.

We first met her in a group activity organized by the EQUAL project at the local disability service provider. To this activity, people were asked to bring along something important to them, and Mary brought a picture of her daughter. We later understood that she only brought a picture of her daughter because her son lives with an aunt from his father's side, who is his legal guardian, and she has not seen him for years.

We met Mary for the second time during our interview. Her mobilization was mediated by the local disability service provider, who arranged a time and made a room available for us. For this interview, Mary came along with her older sister, who is also her legal representative, and the interview was conducted with them both. Mary was very quiet and shy and, therefore, very difficult to interview. At some moments it seemed that she was away in her thoughts, and we tried to involve her as much as possible in the conversation. Her sister, though, was very reactive and available to answer. The interview was, therefore, a continuous exercise of balancing the voices of Mary and her sister and the need to gather the needed information for our research. This was a complex exercise as, with time, memory gets blurred, and dates and events become confused and imprecise. The chronological reordering of events was possible with the access gained to the guardianship process of Mary's legal capacity. Some events narrated may, however, not be in the exact chronological order, but we believe this has no impact on Mary's powerful life narrative. Let's now focus on Mary's story:

Mary's Story

Mary was born in 1984, in a small village of the interior centre of Portugal. She is the second daughter of three children and lived her childhood and young adulthood with her parents and sisters. Mary crawled till very late, reason why her mother decided to go on a pilgrimage to Fátima.[1] She does not know at what age she started to walk but knows that she only developed this skill after her mother's pilgrimage. Faith is, therefore, a central element in her and her parents' lives. Mary only completed the elementary school. Plus, she does not have many memories of her childhood, but remembers that the first four years of school, what corresponds to elementary school in Portugal, were happy times. She recalls with happiness the kindness of her elementary school teacher who, in rainy mornings, used to give her a ride to school. The schoolteacher was also a local person in Mary's village, and on rainy days, on her way to school, she used to ask her to jump on the car so that she did not get soaked. From those days she also recalls the happy moment that was the birth of her younger sister. That period was, however, marked by the death of her paternal grandmother, an event she recalls with sadness.

When Mary was ten years old, she had an accident that resulted in a skull fracture, and sometime later, she was run over by a car. No detailed information was provided about these two events; however, they were key to Mary's family's understanding of her current medical condition and of the changes in Mary's behaviour that apparently became more evident in adolescence. By this behavioural change, the family refers to the emotional fragility, aggressiveness at home and constant episodes of running away from home at the slightest disagreement, without destination, sometimes even with strangers. According to her older sister, who

[1] Fátima is a religious village in the centre of Portugal known for the supposed miracles of the Virgin Mary and, therefore, regarded as a holy place where people go on pilgrimages.

attended the interview as Mary's legal representative, this change in her behaviour may have started immediately after the accidents. At the time, however, no one noticed and, as she stressed, her parents are humble people with low academic qualifications, plus, in those days, there was no school support available. Mary did finish the first four years of elementary school, but failed the fifth year, leaving school the year after. This episode is recalled with mixed feelings by her, on the one hand she felt sorry for not being able to continue at school with the other kids, on the other she felt relieved, as she was afraid of failing another school year. Additionally, on her last year at school Mary started being bullied by a group of boys, mainly through name-calling. She did not understand what they meant by those names, but understood it was insulting and demeaning towards her. These insults did affect her at the time and lessened the sad feelings about dropping school. After leaving school, Mary stayed at home, helping in domestic tasks whenever she was asked and, in her words, hanging around.

Her adolescence marked the beginning of a conflictual relationship with her parents and older sister. According to the latter, Mary's adolescence was a troublesome period, very demanding for her close family. From that period, Mary only recalls the conflict. Mary's sister insisted, though, that the conflict originated in Mary's behaviour, regarded by the family as inadequate and/or bad. This narrative has now been incorporated in Mary's discourse with the expression of regret towards attitudes like "being bad and running away". In Mary's words "they just wanted me to be a good and happy girl [...] but I didn't believe them, I didn't listen to them! [...] and they upset me as much as I upset them!". Mary used to run away from home and leave home without adult permission.

Mary's childhood and adolescence was, also, marked by domestic violence and economic difficulties. Her father, who was the only employed person in the household, had an alcoholic behaviour, and this originated domestic violence at home. As her older sister clarified, money was never abundant at home, and their father only used physical violence towards their mother, never towards them.

At the age of 23, Mary left her parents' home to live with an unknown person for the family, moving to a distant city. This attitude caused great consternation and upset to her family. This relationship ended shortly after, and in September 2008, Mary met and started a new relationship with the future father of her two children. The couple moved to live together in another city, distant from her family. Soon after the beginning of this new relationship, Mary became pregnant with her first child, who was born in August 2009. The birth of her child allowed a family rapprochement, and her parents and sister came to meet the newborn baby and her partner.

The birth of this child triggered, however, the worsening of her mental health condition, and Mary acquired *postpartum* depression. This depression greatly affected her quality of life and impacted the care of her newborn child. After several visits to the local health services, Mary ended up being admitted to a central hospital in Lisbon who established contact with her blood family. Her family was, though, distant and unaware of the general situation. They did know, however, of the financial difficulties of the couple. In fact, Mary, in a moment of despair, called her older sister to explain that they did not have money to buy milk for the baby, as her partner spent all the money they received from the 'newborn child benefit' to buy a new chainsaw and other equipment, leaving the family without money to survive. The financial difficulties of the couple were acute as none of them had a regular employment, had no financial skills to manage the available resources, and Mary's partner already had children from a previous relationship to whom he also had to provide for.

Due to Mary's condition, her need to receive medical treatment, and the inability of the couple to take care and provide for the newborn child, the case was signalled to the local *Commission for the Promotion of the Rights and the Protection of Children and Young People* (CNPDPCJ), an entity in Portugal that monitors the safeguarding and rights of children and young people, and the child was handed over to the care of an aunt, sister of his father. In order to allow the transfer of parental responsibilities during this period of medical treatment, Mary and her partner signed a deal with CNPDPCJ, transferring the parental power to the child's aunt and setting a monthly payment of €200, of which Mary was responsible for the payment of €50, and the father was responsible for the remaining €150. Additionally, this deal established that during this period of medical treatment, Mary was only allowed to see her child for a restricted period of time and always with supervision.

The couple split soon after, and in December 2009, Mary returned to her parents' home in order to get some stability and continue medical treatment to her mental health condition. Mary was, however, very unstable and the distance from her child made her even more unstable. Mary was almost 300Km away from her child, unable to see him. In January 2010, Mary initiated a journey back in order to be close to her baby. Again, Mary got in a very vulnerable situation, without shelter, medical supervision, and medication and was banned from seeing her baby. Once more, in February 2010, Mary was taken to the district hospital in order to receive medical treatment, after which she returned to her parents' home and started receiving support from a local organization for disabled people. Mary stayed at her parents' for a very short period of time as, in May 2010, she had to return to the city where her child was being raised, in order to participate in the court process of parental regulation initiated by the child's aunt. By the end of this process, the parents confirmed the transfer of the parental responsibilities to the child's aunt. Mary did not oppose this decision; her family, however, was not heard in this process. Again, the court decision established a total monthly payment of €200 to support the child's expenses, Mary had to pay €50, and her partner the remaining €150.

The reunion of Mary with her former partner allowed a rapprochement, and soon after the couple resumed the relationship. After receiving a phone call from her partner, Mary once again escaped home to meet him, and both left to a country in Central Europe. As Mary explained, on her arrival, she got a job in agriculture, picking, and packaging peppers in a greenhouse, but she only managed to work a couple of weeks as she immediately got pregnant of her second child, who was born in May 2011, and stopped working. Meanwhile, Mary stopped her medical treatment, and without money, the couple ceased the payments established by the court to support the raising of their first child. This noncompliance with the court's decision had serious consequences in the regulation of the child's parental responsibilities, and Mary lost contact with her son. As she emotionally explained in our conversation, since then, she only saw her son once again when he came to visit and slept over one night at hers and her family's place.

Life in this Central European country was very difficult, and the couple had economic and relational problems. The birth of the couple's second child did not ease the situation, and Mary was abandoned with her six-month-old daughter in a foreign country with no money and no place to live. In December 2011, her partner left for good without them.

In despair, Mary called on her family to ask for help. With the support of her family, in January 2012, Mary and her baby daughter returned to her hometown in Portugal to live at her parents' house. This traumatic experience and the lack of medication and medical support impacted Mary's mental health condition. Mary lost interest in the daily routines and in the care of her daughter. A couple of months after being at her hometown in Portugal, Mary left again to look for her first child. After a couple of days, Mary ended up at the local hospital, diagnosed with mental disorders and was reported to the local authorities as being in danger, as she was living in the streets. Her family was contacted, once again, by the hospital social services and called to intervene. The situation was, however, very difficult as Mary was an adult with free will and the family, with the advice of the hospital social services, contacted the Public Prosecution Service in order to find a solution to bring Mary back home. As Mary was mentally very unstable and in need of medical care, the Public Prosecution Service and the Health Authority established an agreement and issued an arrest warrant [*mandato de condução*]. Mary's older sister arranged with the social services, where Mary was being followed, to have her sent back home by bus. On her arrival, Mary was awaited by the local Health authority and the police and was taken to the psychiatric emergency department and compulsorily hospitalized at the district hospital, for several weeks (April–May 2012), receiving medical treatment. When discharged from the hospital, Mary returned to her parents' home, where she joined her daughter. Mary continued, however, very unstable and continued to leave and return home unattended and without informing anyone. As her sister explained:

Interviewer: Just to understand, when Mary left here, did she leave to meet her partner?

Mary's older sister: With the partner who in this case was no longer … the partner was no longer there, I don't know

	where…, she was more after her son. But when she got there, the doors were blocked…
Interviewer	Okay.
Mary's older sister:	They didn't even let her see her son, nor was she with her partner and she was there for two, or three days, or four, wherever she could.

After a disagreement with her father, Mary initiated another journey back to the place where she used to live with her partner, ending up at the emergency department of the local hospital and, in Jun 2012, she was transferred back to her district hospital to receive medical treatment at the psychiatric service. When discharged from the hospital in July 2012, Mary lived for more than one year (until October 2013) in a shelter run by a local NGO, close to the district hospital. The period after which Mary returned to her parents' house.

Due to Mary's mental health deterioration, her constant journeys back and forward to the place where she used to live with her ex-partner, and repeated episodes at the urgency of health services and, consequently, hospitalizations for medical treatment, Mary's family became very concerned with the stability of her daughter's daily living. According to her older sister, Mary was not taking any medication and was therefore unable to take care of her daughter. The family's main concern was that Mary could take her daughter away without consulting them, putting the minor in danger and them without being able to intervene. As a result, the family initiated a process of regulating parental responsibilities regarding Mary's daughter. At the Parents Meeting [*Conferência de Pais*] held by the court in September 2012, Mary opposed the family's intention. As it is written in the process accessed, and confirmed by Mary in our conversation, she did not want her daughter to stay with her parents, neither with her sister, as she put it:

Interviewer	Yes. I would like to know if Mary, at the beginning of the process, was heard … in the legal action, for example, did the Public Prosecutor's Office hear her?

Mary	I listened. When it came to being the… to pass on family power to my children, I was heard. To my parents, I was heard. Regarding my daughter, I was heard. […]
Interviewer	Did they ask you… your opinion?
Mary	They asked! […] because I even said I didn't want it … I even said I didn't want my daughter in my parents' house. It was my last words, I… that I said. But I wasn't conscious like I am now.
Interviewer	Okay. And do you remember why did you say that? Why did you think that way at the time? […]
Mary	Look, I don't know…
Mary's older sister	It was the head…
Mary	It was the head that wasn't perfect. It wasn't good at those times.
Mary's older sister:	She was not medicated.
Mary	I wasn't medicated; I wasn't at all.

Her ex-partner, the child's father, agreed, however, with the solution, contradicting Mary's will. Less than a month after the Parents' Meeting, Mary underwent psychological assessment at the Institute of Forensic Medicine. The final court decision, announced in September 2013, transferred the parental responsibility of Mary's daughter to her older sister, continuing, though, under the care of her grandparents, with whom the child had lived since she returned from the Central European country. The court decision, also, defined that both parents could freely visit their daughter, and fixed a monthly payment to each parent of €85, to support their daughter's expenses.

Meanwhile, Mary's family was also confronted with court cases initiated by Mary's creditors against her, with a huge debt and with the seizure of her belongings. Mary's and her ex-partner's irregular participation in the job market, money scarcity and the lack of financial literacy translated into the couple's difficulty managing their financial resources and the accumulation of unpaid bills (mostly internet and mobile network suppliers). With time, these unpaid bills piled up with penalties and court expenses resulting from the actions initiated by the creditors. As

Mary was the one signing most of the contracts while living in partnership, she ended up with a large debt and with court decisions seizing her assets. In order to preserve the family's possessions, Mary's family presented a legal process asking for her legal guardianship due to prodigality. This process, initiated in May 2013, ended in January 2015, with Mary's guardianship.

Mary was not totally aware of the court decision, and when asked about it, she redirected the question to her sister. The almost coincidence between this process and the process for regulating the parental responsibilities of her daughter, initiated by her family, confused her. As stated in the report of the psychological forensic assessment that Mary was submitted to during this second process, she believed that the assessment was meant either to get her back to the hospital or to take her children away.

Mary's Interdiction Process

Mary's guardianship process started in May 2013, as a family strategy to sort out her financial problems. As expressed by her sister, the process was intended to disqualify her as capable of managing her finances, due to mental health problems, to cancel all the contracts previously signed, to declare null all the debts resulting from these previous contracts and to reverse the property lien that resulted from court decisions. Moreover, the family wanted the court to designate one of them as Mary's curator, making this person responsible for administrating Mary's finances and belongings.

In October 2013, Mary was summoned by the court to be submitted to a psychological forensic assessment, which took place in March 2014, to determine her cognitive abilities and support the court's decision.

This guardianship/curatorship expertise [*Perícia de Interdição/Inabilitação*] concluded, based on an IQ test conducted by the previous psychological assessment at the Institute of Forensic Medicine, that Mary had a mild-to-moderate cognitive impairment, feeble mind in the original [*debilidade mental*], suggesting that 'guardianship' was the adequate measure for Mary. The final court decision, issued in January 2015, dictated Mary's guardianship and appointed her parents as her legal guardians.

The court decision, issued by the judge in January 2015, was grounded in medical assessments and stated the following facts to be considered in the analysis of the process:

> [...]8. the respondent does not reveal the capacity for abstraction, showing herself to be incapable of interpreting proverbs.
> 9. The respondent MARY has a below average intellectual endowment, having an intelligence quotient of 55, which corresponds to a very high cognitive dysfunction.
> 10. Presents a clinical picture compatible with a diagnosis of mild and moderate mental impairment, requiring support, guidance and assistance especially when subjected to unusual stress.
> 11. The respondent reveals ideoinstinctive thinking, with little planning and without analyzing the consequences and implications of her actions. [...]

This information was transcribed directly from the psychological assessment that Mary was subjected to in 2013 and from the 'guardianship/curatorship expertise' she was subjected to in March 2014.

From these supposed facts, extracted from the medical assessments, the judge deducted the two last facts to be considered for issuing the court decision, based on Article 138 of the Portuguese Civil Code:

> [...] 12. The respondent MARY shows independence in basic activities of daily living (eating, personal hygiene and movement) and lacks full support and supervision in most instrumental activities of daily living, such as shopping appropriately, managing money, caring for and planning her children's needs.
> 13. The respondent appears incapable of governing, based on her own judgment, her person and assets. [...]

Article 138 of the Portuguese Civil Code states that:

> 1. All those who, due to psychic anomaly, deafness or blindness, prove to be incapable of governing their persons and property, may be interdicted from exercising their rights

The judge went on, distinguishing 'guardianship' and 'curatorship', and stating the conditions for issuing a court decision of 'guardianship'. Within these conditions, the court decision states that these anomalies needed to be disabling, present, and permanent, and concluded that what distinguished the two regimes was the severity of impairment and its effects. From this statement, the magistrate dictated that Mary's psychic anomaly was proved, that it was characterized as mild-to-moderate mental impairment, that it was a present condition, that she was unable to govern her life and her assets and concluded that the requirements to call and declare the guardianship regime were met. In the following section of the court decision, the judge stated that the 'guardianship/curatorship expertise' grounded the decision and that it was not contested, thus justifying the immediate imposition of the guardianship regime. Plus, the magistrate appointed Mary's parents as her legal guardians.

Discussion

Mary's case renders visible the limits of law and the fragility of the construction of the former guardianship and curatorship regime. Mary is a testimony to the injustice of the previous regime and of the nullity of the new regime. In fact, Mary's family started a process requesting her 'curatorship' or 'inability' for prodigality, but the judge went even further in his/her decision and aggravated the court decision to the most restrictive regime, i.e. 'guardianship'. This regime imposed, however, huge limits on Mary's legal capacity in the different spheres of her life, beyond the management of economic resources, including sexual and reproductive rights, capacity to marry or establish love relationships, and the exercise of voice and control over all decisions affecting her life. Despite Mary's lack of awareness of the practical consequences of this court decision, her citizenship rights became, and still are, hugely curtailed.

Mary's story is, also, an example of the lack of objectivity of the criminal and court procedures and decisions. Her case reveals the centrality of medical discourses and assessments, the effect of socio-economic conditions and cultural background on medical assessments and court hearings and decisions, the disrespect towards her voice and will and the abusive use of power by the court. Finally, this case reveals that the enforcement of the new Scheme of the Accompanied Adult had no impact on Mary's life nor on her legal capacity, as no changes were made to the limitations introduced by her previous guardianship regime, and no reassessment of the implemented measures was conducted. Her case highlights, thus, the difficulties associated with the regime transition and, above all, the impact this has on people's legal capacity and human rights. The legal capacity reform announced by Law 49/2018 of 14 August remained, thus, invisible to some people with psychosocial impairments, raising concerns about a possible capture of the new law (Krieger, 2003). The perpetuation of the former regime, in spirit and in practice, i.e. in people's perceptions and actions, signifies not only the continuous prevalence of the 'capacity contract' but also the extension of previous challenges and violations of disabled people's rights (Pinto et al., 2023).

Conclusion

Mary currently lives with her daughter and her parents in her hometown. She receives injected medication every single month, plus oral medication, controlled by the local disability service she attends daily in her hometown, and has follow-up medical appointments at the psychiatry service of her district hospital every two months. Mary is also integrated in a long-term care unit run by a local organization for the disabled. This disability NGO, where we met her, is now responsible for Mary's daily and monthly medication intake, for taking her to the medical appointments at the district hospital, for organizing her daily routine, and for her daily transportation to and from home. Mary's routine is now very organized: three days per week she stays at a factory where she prepares catalogues of product samples (fixing the different samples to the catalogue and attaching the respective labels), the other two days she stays at the organization and participates in the different workshops offered there (informatics, cooking, book binding,…). She has, however, no salary resulting from her work at the factory, as this work is framed as 'Socially Useful Activities', and, therefore, considered an occupational answer for disabled people in the real work context, only allowing the training of socio-professional skills. The factory gives her a monthly gratification of approximately €30 to €40 and pays some money directly to her disability organization to support her lunch meals and transport on working days. The definition of this gratification Mary receives from the factory, however, was discretionary, as she voiced in our conversation:

Mary	At the factory I receive around 30 or 40 euros. […]
Interviewer	Per month?
Mary	Yes.
Interviewer	Okay. And do you think this is enough for your work?
Mary	It should be a little more, but we… […] we were two people in the beginning, and the girl who was there, who was called XXX, asked the boss: look, should I give each one 100 euros, or how do I do it? And he said, look… divide that amount and give half for each one, and now it's like this. The other person left, the other boy, and it's like this and I only get these 30 to 40 euros.

Mary is, though, very happy with this experience, and she has a good relationship with people at the factory, evident in the following conversation:

Interviewer	Okay. And do you usually, do you usually speak with? Do you usually […] interact with other people at the factory?
Mary	Yes, yes, yes. They come at 10 am to have breakfast… eat something […] And they speak to me.
Mary's older sister	It's a good, really good connection. When we pass by in the street, they say, look, there comes Mary.
[…]	
Interviewer	How is your relationship with… the people there?
Mary	It's good, yes.

Mary's older sister	It's really good. As incredible as it may seem.
Mary	Sometimes I can't drink coffee, but sometimes they ask: - Mary, have you had breakfast yet? - I took it at home! "- Don't you want a decaf or a coffee?" And I say, "- look, if you want to offer, offer a decaf because I can't have coffee or a *galão [coffee with milk served in a tall glass]*, whatever you want." And then they give me a *galão*, or they give me a decaf, but it's there every once in a while.

Mary is now stable, living with her family, despite the absence of her son, and receiving adequate medical and social support in the community. As her sister expressed during our interview, Mary has been her 'right hand', taking care of her children, an indispensable support when she works in shifts, especially on night shifts. Mary stays home, taking care of the children and providing for their needs. As Mary also shared in the interview, she supports her father when needed in the fields and supports her mother at home when she asks her to cook some meals. She is especially proud of her soup. As her story highlights, adequate support is essential for the well-being and for allowing people to actively participate in their families and society at large. Moreover, Mary's case signals the need to have sentences and diagnoses revised and to reassess the conditions. Mary's case is also paradigmatic of the limits of the legal capacity reform, which remains invisible and with no consequences for some people with psychosocial impairments, perpetuating the former 'capacity contract' and violating people's human and citizenship rights.

References

Krieger, L. H. (2003). Sociolegal Backlash. In L. H. Krieger (Ed.), *Backlash Against the ADA: Reinterpreting Disability Rights* (pp. 340–393). The University of Michigan Press.

Pinto, P. C., Fontes, F., Neca, P., Bento, S., & Alves, J. P. (2023). Rights for All? Living Conditions and (De)citizenship of Adults with Intellectual and Complex Disabilities in Portugal. *Journal of Applied Research in Intellectual Disabilities, 36*(5), 1092–1100. https://doi.org/10.1111/JAR.13128

Open Access This chapter is licensed under the terms of the Creative Commons Attribution 4.0 International License (http://creativecommons.org/licenses/by/4.0/), which permits use, sharing, adaptation, distribution and reproduction in any medium or format, as long as you give appropriate credit to the original author(s) and the source, provide a link to the Creative Commons license and indicate if changes were made.

The images or other third party material in this chapter are included in the chapter's Creative Commons license, unless indicated otherwise in a credit line to the material. If material is not included in the chapter's Creative Commons license and your intended use is not permitted by statutory regulation or exceeds the permitted use, you will need to obtain permission directly from the copyright holder.

7

Samuel's Story—"A process conducted in secrecy": Disability and Symbolic Violence

Teresa Janela Pinto

Abstract Samuel's story recounts a life shaped by poverty, exclusion, and repeated silencing. Born in Lisbon in 1965 to a working-class family, he remembers small joys—bike rides and music—alongside bullying, stigma, and economic strain. After his mother's death, he lost his main support and was institutionalized; secretive legal proceedings led to interdiction, stripping him of rights such as financial autonomy and marriage without a clear explanation. His sister controlled his pension and finances. Samuel internalized silence as a coping strategy against symbolic violence and devaluation, dreaming of revoked interdiction so he might marry, manage his money, and regain dignity and independence.

Interview conducted and analysed by Teresa Janela Pinto.

T. J. Pinto (✉)
Observatory on Disability and Human Rights and Interdisciplinary Centre on Gender Studies, Institute of Social and Political Sciences, University of Lisbon, Lisbon, Portugal
e-mail: teresajpinto@iscsp.ulisboa.pt

© The Author(s) 2026

P. Campos Pinto et al. (eds.), *Equal Rights, Equal Voices*, Palgrave Socio-Legal Studies,
https://doi.org/10.1007/978-3-032-05969-7_7

Keywords Symbolic violence • Guardianship • Devaluation and silencing • Right to marry

Early Years

Samuel was born in 1965. He grew up in a large city, with his parents, older sister, and paternal grandmother. From his most immediate circle, he also remembers a neighbour and his godmother, who, while his mother was alive, "always gave him presents for Christmas and his birthday", but with whom he would end up losing contact over the years.

From this period, which he describes as a "little troubled", he recalls the struggles of his working-class family in the last years of the dictatorship. His mother was a concierge and his father a baker, and while his family managed to get by daily, the financial strain was always present. The duress of this period took a toll on family relationships. He recalls the frugal management of daily expenses in the family, describing his parents as "very stingy with money". Still, he views his relationship with his parents and sister as ambivalent, marked by happy and sad memories, as is the case with "most families".

The rare treats and moments of celebration are recalled with nostalgia and affection. He cherishes the memory of the occasional visits to the popular fair with his parents and sister. Everything from those visits is recalled with pleasure—the savoury and sweet treats, and the joy of the unusual attractions. He smiles at the memory of a cow that poured wine and used to make them laugh as they were kids. The moments of pleasure and freedom in his childhood are also linked to his bike rides, which, he recalls with regret, he had to give up later due to impaired vision. One hobby he managed to keep throughout the years is listening to music. He remembers role-playing with his sister, from an early age, miming the "listener request" programmes that were popular on the radio at the time. They would play along and listen to music on a small Telefunken device. To this day, one of his favourite hobbies remains listening to music and selecting the music for his flatmates on special occasions.

Samuel attended a private special education school through most of his elementary education, from 5 to 14 years old. He has painful memories from this period, saying he never felt happy at that school. He recalls experiencing bullying from a young age. Some colleagues used to call him "jagunço", in a demeaning reference to a character from a Brazilian soap opera that was popular at the time. Samuel recalls the impact of this labelling on his dignity, describing this period of his life as a "hard time". He recalls feeling his dignity and sense of worth diminished not only by his peers' behaviour but also due to the lack of support, indifference and incomprehension he felt from teachers, other school staff and even his family. He believes his complaints regarding how he was treated were not always taken seriously. On occasion, they would separate him from these colleagues, putting them in different classes, but he felt these were mitigated responses to the problem, and the general way he was treated by the teachers and other school staff made him feel he was not important.

Samuel presents this as one of the first of multiple occasions where he felt his words, needs, feelings and actions were received with discredit and distrust. He affirms in a peremptory manner that "my teachers did not support me at all" and believes that this also intersected with class issues, since the students' economic and social capital played a part in the way students were treated at the time:

Samuel: They only cared about the "jobs for the boys"
Interviewer: Students with more social capital?
Samuel: Yes.

After leaving that school, Samuel would attend multiple disability service providers, in professional training and occupational activities. In total, he recalls attending five different service providers up to his adult years, although the precise periods remain uncertain in his memory. He has fond recollections of doing professional training in weaving and macrame, and the chance of doing some paid work in that area, although he no longer remembers how much he earned at the time. He has trouble recalling some details of this period, as it happened "a long time ago" and presents a broad overview of the organizations he attended and some of the activities he used to take part in. He also says he does not want to dwell on memories of those places, although he recalls with sorrow the same sense of being discredited, reproduced on different occasions when his word was questioned.

In two organizations, he was accused of stealing. When he was doing training as a telephone operator, they accused him of stealing a phone. Later, in another association, they accused him of stealing a teacher's food. He remembers this with a hurtful tone and stops speaking at this moment. When he resumes, he says they would not trust his word, recalling the sense of injustice, accruing to the notion that his dignity and value as a person were not deemed important. He says he developed, in time, a coping strategy to deal with this discredit and discrimination. By keeping to himself and sharing as little as possible, he learned he would not be as exposed to this form of violence. Even when discriminated against, he states he does not usually share it with anyone, because "sometimes silence is the best thing".

Legal Proceedings

Samuel's institutionalization process and legal proceedings regarding legal capacity were initiated in the same period, after his mother's death. His father died in 1996. By the time his mother passed away, a decade later, he had lost contact with other significant figures in his life, and the sole support he received was from his sister, who was already married at the time. He went to live with his sister, brother-in-law and nephews for a time. His brother-in-law had chronic health conditions that required attention, and when his own sister had health concerns of her own, it became too much to manage, as he recalls.

> My mother died and my sister needed to be relieved. She looked for several places, until she found [name of the service-provider]. (…) When my sister had an ear surgery I came here, initially for a small period, in 2010, and afterwards, since 2012.[1]

[1] Samuel now attends a different disability service provider.

It was one of the technical directors at the disability service provider he attended at the time that first talked to his sister about the possibility of starting legal proceedings for tutelage under the previous legal capacity regime. He says he is not acquainted with the reasons evoked in the initial petition.[2] They told him what would happen very briefly, stating it was for his security and best interest, and his sister agreed.

The perception that his voice and value were not considered significant reached its apex during these legal proceedings. Although he has a scarce recollection of the details of the process, he recalls feeling deeply unsettled by the legal process, where his opinion and wishes were not considered.

Samuel: I felt bad. (...) Sad...
Interviewer: About the final decision or about the way the process was conducted?
Samuel: About everything! About everything! I didn't say so at the time but...
Interviewer: You didn't tell that to [your sister] at the time?
Samuel: No. And neither would she care explain it to me...it was a process conducted in secrecy!

Perhaps due to this lack of involvement and the painful memory it evokes, Samuel does not want to dwell on memories of the court proceedings but prefers to discuss how he views the sentence and its impact on his life. The court decision applied the most restrictive sentence under the previous regime, *interdiction*. The sentence imposed several restrictions on personal rights, including the right to manage financial assets and to marry. He remembers being informed of the decision, without an effort to explain the court ruling and its full implications:

[2] It was not possible to have access to the court documents of Samuel's legal capacity process. Despite multiple requests by the researchers and the technical director at Samuel's current disability service provider, the family stated they could not find his court sentence and other supporting documents. For this reason, details regarding the reasons evoked in the initial petition and the exact restrictions imposed on his legal rights by the court sentence are reconstructed through Samuel's life narrative, rather than through the precise wording of the court documents.

> No one explained it to me, no one! They just said: "that's it, you're interdicted". They did not bother to explain anything else…

Samuel receives an invalidity pension, though he does not have a precise idea of its value. He has no access to the bank account. His sister manages this money and makes a monthly transfer to the disability service provider that he attends. There, they give him a small weekly allowance for regular expenses. Despite stating that he receives enough money for his regular expenses, and that he can request for more money—for instance, if going out for lunch on special occasions—Samuel says he wished he could have more financial independence.

Samuel: Being able to receive the money. Have a debit card…
Interviewer: You don't have autonomy for that?
Samuel: No.

The court sentence did not restrict his voting rights. Samuel says he is very interested in politics, and it is important for him to vote. He usually votes for the same centre-left-wing party, which he links to his family background and consciousness of social rights:

> I'm a left-wing voter. For the right, we had enough with Salazar![3]

Yet, the full scope of the restriction of his personal rights would only become fully visible years later. He met Florence in his previous residence in 2016. After dating for a few years, they wanted to marry. He says he was apprehensive before talking to his sister about the possibility of marriage, but says he received support from his colleagues and staff in the organization he attends.

Samuel: I was a little scared.
Interviewer: Why?

[3] António de Oliveira Salazar was the central figure of the *Estado Novo* (1933–1974), Portugal's authoritarian regime, ideologically aligned with the authoritarian right, and marked by conservative Catholicism and nationalism. He served as President of the Council of Ministers from 1932 to 1968, exercising tight control over both the government and society throughout his tenure.

Samuel: I'm not sure why…
Interviewer: Were you in some way fearing she would not approve of the decision?
Samuel: Yes.
Interviewer: And how did the other people around you react?
Samuel: Here [in the organisation he attends] they reacted well.
Interviewer: They supported your decision?
Samuel: Yes.

Samuel explained that he only learned from his sister that the court ruling prohibited him from marrying. When asked what he was told at the time about the possibility of marriage, he replied, "That I couldn't". Upon further questioning about who informed him of this restriction, he explained that it was his sister, confirming that it was one of the personal rights that was restricted in the court ruling. Samuel admitted that he had not been aware of this restriction beforehand, stating "There are things they keep from me, I don't know why…" When asked how this made him feel, he expressed sadness and resignation, stating "What choice did I have?!"

To date, not being able to get legally married and getting married in a church as was their wish remains one of Samuel's greatest regrets. As suggested by some of the staff at their residence, Samuel and Florence had a symbolic wedding ceremony to mark their union. He cherishes the memory of the ceremony that took part on the same day as his birthday seven years ago. No family members attended, but some colleagues were present. When recalling moments of happiness, he highlights his wedding ceremony and honeymoon, where he and his wife stayed in a hotel in Lisbon.

Despite the lack of legal recognition of the marriage, Samuel addresses Florence as his wife. When at the start of the interview, he briefly mentions her and we ask if she is his girlfriend, he promptly corrects us and states "she is my wife". Still, the symbolic wedding ceremony conducted by friends and colleagues did not diminish Samuel's wish to see his sentence revised and be able to be legally married, as a full citizen, something that, together with the reversal of the court ruling, is presented as his biggest dream.

Interviewer: What things do you wish you could do but are unable to [due to the sentence]?
Samuel: I would like to get married in church.

Later Life

Samuel currently lives in a supported living facility. Though he no longer lives in the same residence as his wife, he says they meet very often, especially during the weekends, and talk regularly on the phone. Samuel states they sometimes go for a walk with other people from the organization, but also manage to spend time alone, and occasionally stay out for lunch.

Even today, he sees no reason for the sentence and provides examples of his capacity and agency. Samuel describes his routine in his supported care home, stating he does multiple tasks, mostly during the weekends, since he has classes during the weekdays. He helps with the general household chores, such as doing the laundry, preparing meals and other tasks. He is particularly proud of having returned to school to finish basic education. He attends a public school during the evenings. He is now completing eighth grade in an Adult Education and Training Program. Samuel contrasts the negative experiences of his early school years with the positive integration in the new school:

Samuel: Since I'm in this school, I prefer not to remember the previous ones and focus on this one. Here…I'm learning! I have access to lectures, we do study trips (…) [I study] Portuguese, English, Maths, Citizenship and Computer Sciences.
Interviewer: And are you enjoying it?
Samuel: Yes.

Samuel describes a charged weekly schedule, especially during the weekdays. He wakes up very early to go to the socio-occupational forum he attends during the day. Mid-afternoon, he goes to school and returns home around 10 or 11 p.m. after his classes. He commutes every day using multiple transports by himself.

Looking back on the legal proceedings and what he wished to have happened differently, he shares:

Interviewer: What did you wish had happened differently?
Samuel: Not having an interdiction.
Interviewer: How do you feel about the effect of the interdiction in your daily life?
Samuel: The saddest thing is … it's this interdiction!
Interviewer: What are the things that you wish you could do but cannot? Earlier, you mentioned that you had a dream of getting married.
Samuel: Yes! That and having a bank card to manage my money.
Interviewer: (…) What are your dreams and projects for the future. If you could, what would be the first thing you would change in your life?
Samuel: Getting married. (…) and having a house.

Samuel says his happiest moment will be when the court sentence is revoked. There was no indication, at the time of writing, that a process for sentence revision had been initiated.

Comment

This chapter drew on an in-depth biographical interview conducted with Samuel, a nearly 60-year-old man with visual and psychosocial impairment. Samuel's story first came to our attention when he took part in a focus group with persons with psychosocial disabilities, where Samuel had the chance to share part of his story and the effects of legal capacity restriction on his personal rights. This interview explored his life story, recalling meaningful events and crossroads through the life course.

Samuel's life is marked by silences and omissions—in his personal life and interaction with others, but also in his court proceedings. As previously stated, it was not possible to access the court documents concerning his legal capacity process, which are in the possession of a family member, who does not know its whereabouts. Despite the difficulties in scheduling the interview and delay in obtaining authorization—legally required—from his sister, Samuel wanted to make his voice heard and proceed with the biographical interview. He does so, however, in a reserved way, clearly identifying what he wants to share. Given Samuel's trajectory and how he frames the role of silence and reservedness as a coping mechanism against the threat of discredit for his word and violation of his sense of dignity and self-worth that he says he experienced throughout his life, we were especially attentive to the need to listen to Samuel's story and tell the story of his life, in his own words, without pressing for additional material and corroboration. Respect for his will and timing was a constant concern in the collection of all the life stories included in this book, but it took even greater meaning in this interview, as Samuel traced his story.

Samuel's story illustrates how pervasive negative social representations of disability and mental health contribute to a life trajectory marked by labelling, mistrust, concealments and other forms of symbolic violence, conceived as the relations and forms of domination and power that do not stem from obvious physical force or violence (Bourdieu, 2002).

From a childhood marked by some happy memories of child play and occasional family outings, as well as the harshness of the living conditions of his working-class family, Samuel's more pervasive and negative memory is connected to experiences of bullying in school. In some cases, bullying overlaps with stigma and discrimination, targeting students who are already in a marginalized position, further contributing to their exclusion, and the responses of teachers and significant others help to signal what is an acceptable and an unacceptable behaviour (Njelesani et al., 2022). Discredit and lack of support may thus convey and shape notions regarding the person's symbolic status, dignity and worth. Questioning the credibility of persons with disabilities' accounts of discrimination and violence has important impacts on their sense of worth (Wiseman & Watson, 2022) and constitutes a violation of their legitimacy and social status, which lies at the core of the concept of symbolic violence.

This notion that he was somewhat deemed less worthy persisted throughout Samuel's youth and adulthood, reinforced in personal and institutional encounters where he felt he was not acknowledged. The silence imposed on him by withdrawing important information from him, including during the procedures that resulted in his legal capacity sentence, was internalized in time as a strategy to cope with delegitimization and mistrust. As Swartz et al. (2018, p. 26) argue, to "counter, manage and defend against others' devaluations' persons with disabilities must employ a variety of strategies (…) in order to hide, minimise, compensate for, or negate the socially stigmatised elements of their identities". Samuel describes how he learned to stay silent as a strategy to cope with reiterated experiences of discrediting and mistrust. The protection of his identity and dignity comes at a cost of silencing his voice and certain aspects of his identity in public, thus reinforcing the "symbolic violence of effacement" (Swartz et al., 2018, p. 27) experienced by Samuel and many persons with disabilities.

The court sentence that limited the exercise of his legal capacity, imposing restrictions on his right to be married, or to manage his financial assets, was perceived by Samuel as yet another instance of symbolic violence, where he endured denial of his agency, personhood and access to rights. Structures of domination can be produced both in everyday practices and interactions, such as in the bullying, and discredit Samuel endured, but also through legal and political discourses and practices that reproduce that unequal status, in the "macropolitics of institutional silencing" (Morgan & Björkert, 2006, p. 448).

While Samuel's case exemplifies both micro and macro forms of symbolic violence, it also demonstrates how restrictions on personal rights, as imposed through the court ruling on legal capacity, can be particularly insidious. These restrictions are legitimized by institutions and figures with formal authority, making them more likely to be accepted as dominant representations and institutional norms. However, although Samuel employs coping strategies, such as deliberate silencing, to navigate both personal and institutional symbolic violence, this should not be interpreted as a tacit acceptance of his unequal status. Samuel remains acutely aware of the injustice and unequal power dynamics at play, and he continues to hope for the reversal of the sentence with the eventual recognition of his marriage.

References

Bourdieu, P. (2002). *Language and Symbolic Power*. Polity Press.

Morgan, K., & Björkert, S. T. (2006). "I'd rather you'd lay me on the floor and start kicking me": Understanding Symbolic Violence in Everyday Life. *Women's Studies International Forum, 29*(5), 441–452. https://doi.org/10.1016/j.wsif.2006.07.002

Njelesani, J., Lai, J., Gigante, C. M., & Trelles, J. (2022). Will You Protect Me or Make the Situation Worse?: Teachers' Responses to School Violence Against Students With Disabilities. *Journal of Interpersonal Violence, 37*(23–24), NP21723–NP21748. https://doi.org/10.1177/08862605211062996

Swartz, L., Hunt, X., Watermeyer, B., Carew, M., Braathen, S. H., & Rohleder, P. (2018). Symbolic Violence and the Invisibility of Disability. *African Safety Promotion, 16*(2), 21–30.

Wiseman, P., & Watson, N. (2022). Because I've Got a Learning Disability, They Don't Take Me Seriously. *Violence, Wellbeing, and Devaluing People With Learning Disabilities., 37*, 13–14. https://doi.org/10.1177/0886260520990828

Open Access This chapter is licensed under the terms of the Creative Commons Attribution 4.0 International License (http://creativecommons.org/licenses/by/4.0/), which permits use, sharing, adaptation, distribution and reproduction in any medium or format, as long as you give appropriate credit to the original author(s) and the source, provide a link to the Creative Commons license and indicate if changes were made.

The images or other third party material in this chapter are included in the chapter's Creative Commons license, unless indicated otherwise in a credit line to the material. If material is not included in the chapter's Creative Commons license and your intended use is not permitted by statutory regulation or exceeds the permitted use, you will need to obtain permission directly from the copyright holder.

8

Sophie's Story—"Minus ten!": When the Law Hears, But Does Not Listen

Teresa Janela Pinto

Abstract Sophie's story traces a supportive childhood: despite challenges, she enjoyed school, learned practical skills, and built strong family bonds. As an adult, she benefits from a personal assistant through the Independent Living Support Scheme, which helps her manage daily tasks, produce YouTube cooking videos, attend internships, and pursue social activities such as swimming and the gym. Legal proceedings aimed at assigning

This case was analysed by Teresa Janela Pinto, based on multiple sources. At Sophie's request, the interview was conducted by someone she knew. She chose her personal assistant to support her by reading aloud the pre-sent questions and recording her responses, which were videotaped and transcribed. Additional materials included documents from the legal proceedings—such as the initial petition, the filing by the Prosecutor General's Office, the court ruling, and email exchanges with judicial actors—provided by the family. The analysis also drew on an interview with Sophie's mother, conducted within the framework of Project EQUAL.

T. J. Pinto (✉)
Observatory on Disability and Human Rights and Interdisciplinary Centre on Gender Studies, Institute of Social and Political Sciences, University of Lisbon, Lisbon, Portugal
e-mail: teresajpinto@iscsp.ulisboa.pt

© The Author(s) 2026

P. Campos Pinto et al. (eds.), *Equal Rights, Equal Voices*, Palgrave Socio-Legal Studies,
https://doi.org/10.1007/978-3-032-05969-7_8

support, however, focused on her deficits, and the lack of communication adjustments severely constrained Sophie's autonomy. Sophie's case illustrates the persistence of the individual model of disability in court proceedings, which prioritises clinical diagnoses and equates legal capacity with cognitive capacity, overlooking how supportive environments can enable individuals to exercise their rights.

Keywords Individual model of disability • Personal assistance • Guardianship • Supportive environments

Early Years

Sophie was born in 1997 in one of Portugal's largest cities. The pregnancy was closely monitored due to complications related to maternal hypertension and advanced maternal age. She is the youngest of the siblings, and grew up with her parents, brother, and sister, spending her childhood between the family's homes in two cities.

Sophie says she felt very loved as she grew up. Her parents, siblings, and other significant figures in her life engaged with her frequently, fostering a strong sense of connection. That protective family network reached her extended family and, even today, she keeps a close bond with her aunt and her godmother. She remembers they would give her many kisses and gifts on special occasions.

At the age of two, Sophie began attending preschool in a private institution. Around the same time, some concerns regarding her psychomotor developmental delay arose. Sophie's mother, who is a nurse, encouraged the paediatrician to investigate the situation more thoroughly. This ultimately led to a genetic assessment, which identified a rare chromosomal deletion.

Sophie later attended kindergarten and primary school at a different private institution, and she still remembers the names of her teachers. After completing primary school, she transitioned to a local public school for middle school.

Sophie holds joyful memories of her school years, valuing both the learning process and the sense of accomplishment that came with it.

Sophie particularly enjoyed acquiring practical skills, such as learning how to navigate shopping trips, which she later applied in everyday situations, including going out for coffee or engaging in similar activities.

As is often the case during adolescence, Sophie went through a phase of increased independence and defiance, wanting to make her own choices. She occasionally clashed with her parents, particularly over her desire to spend more time on the internet, which they tried to regulate.

Sophie's interactions with fellow students evolved over the years. During kindergarten and primary school, her peers frequently included her in their play. However, in the larger settings of public middle and high schools, social integration became more challenging. She often spent her time accompanied by a teacher or auxiliary staff. Sophie recalls that she did not have many friends during this period and was rarely invited to parties, though she also remembers moments of warmth and care. One of her most cherished memories is receiving a heart-shaped pillow from her classmates on her 14th birthday, which she still keeps in her bedroom. Despite the social challenges, Sophie felt that her teachers and school staff genuinely liked and cared for her.

Overall, Sophie regards her school years as a happy period in her life. However, she recalls one particularly sad moment when she saw her mother crying because she had initially been denied admission to a school. Eventually, she was able to attend the same high school, where she completed her formal education. She benefited from adaptations to the school curriculum through an Individualized Specific Curriculum, which enabled her to complete the 12 years of compulsory education.

Adulthood

After completing school, Sophie initially stayed at home before enrolling in professional training for a period. She also attended a Centre of Occupational Activities (CAO), which would later be transformed into a Centre of Activities and Empowerment for Inclusion (CACI). Later, she started being supported by a personal assistant through the Independent Living Support Scheme.[1]

Sophie continued to work with her personal assistant, developing multiple skills, such as managing household chores, running errands to the grocery store and other locations, and engaging in various tasks and activities. She also attended a study support centre, which she enjoyed because it kept her engaged.

Following her professional training, Sophie had the opportunity to gain work experience through short-term internships in the open labour market. She completed internships in a laundry, a grocery store, and a supermarket, handling tasks such as folding clothes, restocking shelves, and pricing items. During her time at the large supermarket, Sophie developed good rapport with her colleagues. She felt liked and appreciated, even though, at times, she would "make a scene" by speaking loudly or shouting. She acknowledges that her colleagues and supervisors struggled to understand these moments, and she herself was unable to explain what triggered them. Despite this, Sophie has fond memories of these work experiences.

Sophie states that she has never felt discriminated against because of her disability. However, she recalls an incident when she was excluded from a vacation programme organized by the local parish. The programme, which offered various recreational and creative activities for children and young people, refused to allow Sophie to participate, prompting the family to file a complaint for discrimination on the grounds of disability. Her mother notes that Sophie tends to be somewhat "in her own world", which may protect her from being affected by such instances.

Politics is not something Sophie expresses an interest in, although she voted in the last elections for the national assembly. Sophie cares about human rights, protection of the environment and animal rights. She tries to pay attention to conversations at home, to see which parties are more aligned with those ideas, and to know who to vote for. She marks the

[1] MAVI—Modelo de Apoio à Vida Independente (Independent Living Support Scheme) is a Portuguese public policy that provides personal assistance to promote autonomy and community participation for persons with disabilities.

ballot herself, although she relies on support to fold it and place it in the ballot box.

Sophie does not know how much she receives every month, from work or social benefits, and does not express an interest in knowing. She receives every month, in her bank account, the Social Benefit for Inclusion.[2] Usually, the money is managed by her parents. She owns a debit card that she can use, although she does not use it alone. When she wants money for any activity, she asks her parents, although she rarely asks for much.

Sophie says she does not have a boyfriend, although her mother and personal assistant sometimes ask her about it. One of her favourite activities is navigating online. Though her parents say she spends too much time on the Internet, Sophie likes browsing and proudly states that she can type very fast on the computer.

Initial Petition

The initial petition for special accompaniment measures was submitted under the new legal regime. In 2020, following the first wave of the COVID-19 pandemic, a period marked by significant uncertainty and strict restrictions on hospital visits, Sophie's parents grew concerned that they might not be allowed to accompany her in the event of hospital admission. As a result, in September 2020, they initiated legal proceedings under the Accompanied Adult Law. The family initially expected that all of Sophie's personal rights would be maintained and that her mother, as the designated support person, would be permitted to assist—rather than replace—Sophie in the exercise of her rights and duties.

The initial petition submitted by Sophie's mother on her behalf included a list of tasks that the intended beneficiary could or could not perform. The form allowed only yes-or-no responses, but Sophie's family

[2] The Social Benefit for Inclusion (*Prestação Social para a Inclusão*) is a financial support aimed at promoting the autonomy and social inclusion of adults with disabilities. Eligible individuals must have a certified disability degree of 60% or higher. As of 2025, the benefit comprises a base component of up to €324.55 per month for individuals aged 18 and over. An additional supplement of up to €564.98 per month may be granted, depending on the beneficiary's economic situation.

attempted to provide additional context by including notes in some sections—clarifying, for example, that Sophie was able to carry out certain activities with minimal support, such as finding her way in the street or going shopping.

The tasks that Sophie was able to perform included basic orientation in time and space, dressing, reading, writing, counting, performing simple calculations, and holding basic conversations. On the other hand, she was unable to complete certain activities independently, such as going to medical appointments alone, managing money, or attending to personal hygiene without assistance.

In her interview, Sophie's mother clarified that the support Sophie requires is generally limited to communication—providing clear, accessible information to help her make decisions—and occasional feedback on routine tasks to reinforce autonomy. This might include reminders to rinse the shampoo thoroughly or to pace herself while eating. Such support is minimal, aimed at helping Sophie monitor and adjust her actions and gradually build confidence and independence in daily activities. These aspects were communicated by the family, both in the written documentation and later during the expert assessment.

To give a fuller picture of Sophie's abilities, her mother also listed in the initial petition several household chores she performs autonomously, including loading and unloading the dishwasher, vacuuming, dusting, hanging laundry to dry, and folding clothes.

The documentation submitted with the petition included a medical report stating Sophie has a genetic condition that can cause developmental delay and that this condition, though chronic, is non-progressive, so "cognitively, there is no deterioration, so it is expected that [Sophie] will continue to make progress, albeit at her own pace". Another report, from Sophie's paediatrician, specialized in neurodevelopment, dated from July 2020, states that she has an intellectual developmental disorder, autism spectrum disorder, and attention deficit hyperactivity disorder.

Legal Proceedings

The proceedings advanced swiftly. Sophie was summoned to the Procurator General's Office during the instruction phase of the proceedings. Although she was heard, no procedural accommodations were made (United Nations, 2020). The communication was not adapted to Sophie's needs, and the brief exchange failed to establish trust or a genuine understanding. This left Sophie's mother with the impression that although they technically heard Sophie, they neither truly listened nor made any effort to engage with her in a meaningful way. As a result, the image conveyed to the Prosecutor General's Office was that of a person with severely limited capacities.

The Prosecutor General's Office filed the Supported Assistance Action in November 2020. The petition opens by identifying the beneficiary's name and age, immediately citing her medical diagnosis and degree of impairment. It goes on to claim that "the beneficiary's mental and physical impairment is severe and irreversible, rendering her completely incapable of managing her personal affairs and administering her assets".

The Prosecutor General's Office action proceeds to detail everything that Sophie is unable to do, reproducing exclusively the negative elements of the initial request, with no mention whatsoever of tasks Sophie can do autonomously or with minimal supervision. It states that "although the beneficiary can speak, she can only maintain a very basic and simple conversation", "only understands simple instructions and is unable to comprehend what doctors tell her". It also states that Sophie "is not capable of performing even basic arithmetic calculations", here contradicting the information provided by the family in the initial petition, and though "she knows what money is used for (...) cannot assign it value (...) [and] is unable to go shopping alone".

As a result, it concludes that she "requires and depends on third-party supervision 24 hours a day, including for meal preparation, hygiene supervision, and ensuring medication intake, as she is unable to manage these tasks on her own".

With this exclusive focus on areas of impairment, and a notion that equates capacity and autonomy to having no need for any type of support, however minimal, the filing states that the "beneficiary is entirely incapable of surviving without the permanent support of another person, being, in short, permanently and irreversibly completely unable to care for herself and her assets". The Prosecutor General's Office (Filing Action, Section B, Articles 18 and 19; emphasis in original) concludes that:

> Notwithstanding the principle of necessity, set forth in Article 145(1) of the Civil Code, which limits the extent of legal support to the minimum necessary, given the beneficiary's health condition, it is deemed appropriate in this specific case to apply the measure of **general representation**, with full administration of assets (...). Furthermore, considering the beneficiary's clinical condition and her lack of cognitive capacity to make decisions and choices personally and consciously, we find it equally necessary to **limit her strictly personal rights, which do not allow legal representation, namely her personal right to marry or establish a common-law partnership, to travel within the country or abroad, to establish domicile and residence, and to make a will** (...)."

In response to the proposed action, Sophie's mother submitted a formal objection to the Prosecutor General's Office via email in December 2020. In it, she raised concerns after reviewing the initial petition, pointing out inaccuracies and omissions in the way Sophie's abilities and support needs were portrayed.

She particularly contested the framing of Sophie's condition, writing:

> There is no 'state of physical debilitation' [as stated in paragraph 5], and the notion of mental debilitation is debatable. I propose replacing this paragraph with what is stated in the medical report: 'The condition is non-progressive, the organic prognosis is favourable; cognitively, there is no deterioration, so it is expected that [Sophie] will continue to make progress, albeit at her own pace.'

The objection also offered concrete examples of tasks that Sophie was said to be unable to perform independently but could, in fact, carry out with minimal support. Finally, Sophie's mother questioned the overall coherence of the Prosecutor General's filing with both the Accompanied

Adult Law and Article 12 of the CRPD. She emphasized the law's purpose of supporting decision-making rather than replacing it, stating:

> [The] objective is for the person with a disability to be the primary decision-maker and to have specific and personal support to exercise their legal capacity (...). As a mother and an active citizen advocating for my daughter's inclusion in society, it is concerning to see that the application of a law that should ensure equal recognition before the law is instead being used to restrict her rights.

Despite the clarity and relevance of this objection, it was never considered in the court analysis. In March 2021, Sophie underwent a medico-legal assessment at a local public hospital. The encounter reinforced the family's perception that no meaningful effort was made to build rapport or establish a supportive environment for Sophie. During the medico-legal assessment, the expert failed to adapt their communication or interact with her in a way that made her feel at ease. As her mother later noted, "when there's no attempt to connect with Sophie, she simply doesn't engage — she doesn't care who's in front of her or the implications of her answers". The assessment focused exclusively on deficits—what Sophie could not do—while ignoring her abilities, preferences, and support strategies. As Sophie recalls, someone "asked some questions, and I didn't answer. Mother said that the questions are asked the same way for everyone, and that won't do".

In July 2021, owing to concerns over the lack of contact with and information regarding the court-appointed lawyer, Sophie's mother contacted the court. She then received a written communication stating the lawyer's name. It was only then that they learned that the court-appointed lawyer had been assigned to the case in December 2020, but had never contacted Sophie or her family and had already issued legal opinions on the case, supporting the Prosecutor General's Office request, without ever speaking to Sophie or her family.

Court Ruling

The court ruling was issued in October 2021. In its reasoning, the document reproduces the arguments evoked in the Prosecutor General's Office action, focusing exclusively on the medical diagnosis, level of incapacity, irreversibility of the "pathology" to the conclusion that it "compromises the intellectual capacity to understand, decide, and care for herself, making her highly dependent on third-party care and incapable of managing her own affairs and assets".

The ruling concludes that:

> [The] Beneficiary requires a support measure, specifically general representation by a Support Person, with full administration of her assets (…). Given the severity of her condition, the following personal rights of the Beneficiary shall be restricted — marriage or establishment of a common-law partnership, choosing living arrangements, traveling within the country or abroad, making a will, and choosing a profession, as well as entering ordinary transactions of daily life."

Regarding the will of the beneficiary, the court ruling details that a "Public Defender was appointed who, once cited, declared that they did not wish to submit a response as they agreed with the Applicant [Prosecutor General's Office]", and since there was no "opposition from the Prosecutor General's Office and the Beneficiary, represented by the appointed Public Defender, I waive the Beneficiary's hearing".

In the initial petition, the family requested Sophie's mother to be appointed as the support person, and her father and brother as additional support persons, as part of the "family council". This request was respected in the final court decision.

The court ruling was delivered to Sophie's parents by mail. When asked to rate the decision and how it was explained to her on a scale from 1 to 10, Sophie responded with "minus ten!" expressing deep dissatisfaction with how the process was handled. Her family also strongly opposed the ruling, viewing it as a barrier to Sophie's access to her rights. Their frustration was particularly directed at the fact that the public defender and the judge never met Sophie or her family, effectively disregarding her legal right to be heard.

Sophie's mother recalls that, although the court-appointed lawyer later acknowledged that an appeal might be possible due to procedural violations, namely the fact that Sophie had not been heard in court, the lawyer questioned whether it would be worthwhile. Combined with emotional exhaustion and uncertainty about the potential financial costs, the family ultimately chose not to appeal. Later, through disability rights networks, they learned that they would have been entitled to cost exemption, an information they felt had not been properly communicated by the court-appointed lawyer.

Afterword

Concerning the impact of the sentence on Sophie's life, her family explained that they have made a conscious effort to maintain routines and keep her daily life as consistent as possible with how it was before the court decision. While the ruling imposed significant legal restrictions, they have continued to support Sophie in exercising autonomy in her everyday activities. At the same time, they remain attentive to how the decision might affect her rights going forward, particularly in areas such as voting, where the court ruling is silent, leaving the family uncertain about how her participation will be handled in future elections.

Sophie continues to live with her parents. Each day, with the support of her personal assistant, she decides what she wants to do and plans the day's activities. Sophie describes some of her favourite activities:

> I take a dark latte, as it helps with my attention. I go to the library to get books to train my reading. Sometimes I stay there longer doing some worksheets. I do a shopping list and go to the supermarket. I bake cakes and other recipes that I publish in YouTube. Delicious recipes!

Sophie has been running a YouTube channel for some years, where she shares videos of her "delicious" recipes, focusing primarily on healthy savoury and sweet snacks. With the assistance of her personal assistant,

Sophie records and uploads the videos to her channel. She has created over 50 videos showcasing her culinary skills. In addition to cooking, Sophie is also involved in the video production process, with the support of her personal assistant.

> [name of her personal assistant] records the images and helps me post it online, but I'm the one who writes everything, and I like writing on the computer.

Sophie goes to the gym and enjoys swimming. She helps with household chores and likes to spend her free time online. She enjoys going to the cinema, taking walks, having picnics, and spending time with her godmother, siblings, and nephews. Although she is not currently working, she hopes to do another internship in the open labour market. Her mother recalls using her status as a support person only once—when the employment centre refused to provide information about Sophie's registration.

She hopes to continue to rely on the support of her personal assistant as part of the Independent Living Support Scheme. When questioned about what limits her rights, Sophie found it hard to answer, as this draws on abstract notions of rights and self-determination but provided several examples of what she likes and does not like to do, and clearly expressed her wishes:

> Being in places where people my age and of different ages are, having my family, living in my own home, working from home or elsewhere. Feeling the love and protection of family and friends… and having [her personal assistant]'s support so I can let my parents have their own lives. (…) Live every day in a happy way!

Comment

This chapter examines the experience of Sophie, a 27-year-old woman, subjected to a general support measure under the new Accompanied Adult Law. Drawing primarily on the interview with Sophie, complemented by documents from her legal case, and an interview with her mother, it was possible to trace how her legal capacity process was handled.

Diagnosed with a genetic condition affecting her neurodevelopment, Sophie has, nonetheless, learned to read, write, count, and manage daily activities with minimal support. She completed compulsory education and professional training, demonstrating significant personal achievements. Her supportive family has consistently worked to ensure that she exercises her rights and responsibilities like any other person. Until the COVID-19 pandemic, there had been no perceived need for formal support measures. However, the uncertainty brought about by the pandemic led them to seek legal recognition of her right to access support if needed. What followed was a swift but highly bureaucratic legal process that failed to uphold the principles of Article 12 of the CRPD and the intended spirit of the Accompanied Adult Law.

Firstly, court documents in Sophie's case illustrate the persistence of a medical model of disability, prioritizing clinical diagnoses and equating legal capacity with cognitive capacity. This narrow focus on cognitive ability and complex reasoning and communication is particularly detrimental to persons with intellectual disabilities (Arstein-Kerslake, 2017).

Secondly, the court-appointed lawyer never contacted Sophie or her family, failing to represent her interests. Sophie was not heard in court, and no reasonable or procedural accommodations (United Nations, 2020) were provided when she was heard by the Prosecutor General's Office or during the medico-legal assessment.

Thirdly, autonomy and decision-making are dynamic, interactive processes, where the relationship between the individual, the support persons, and the context plays a central role (Fallon-Kund et al., 2017). The criteria used to assess Sophie's legal capacity equated capacity with full autonomy, overlooking how supportive environments enable individuals to exercise their rights. As Arstein-Kerslake (2016, p. 80) argues:

> Article 12 (…) asks for a system where an individual is not denied legal capacity, but provided with the means to exercise that legal capacity. None of us exercise legal capacity alone or in a vacuum. We take support from all around us – our friends, families, experts and professionals.

Balancing protection and respect for autonomy is a complex legal and procedural issue. However, safeguarding the person's best interests must not violate the principles of proportionality and rights protection enshrined in Article 12 of the CRPD (Devi et al., 2011; Fallon-Kund et al., 2017; Holness, 2014) and the Accompanied Adult Law.

Sophie's case illustrates the persistent challenges in translating reforms into practice. While the Accompanied Adult Law represents a significant step forward, the spirit of the new law has not yet been fully internalized by the judiciary. This case highlights the urgent need for a deeper transformation in legal and judicial practices, one that fully embraces the normative shift introduced by the Accompanied Adult Law and Article 12 of the CRPD. This includes a firm commitment to ensuring the right to be heard and implementing reasonable and procedural accommodations (United Nations, 2020), so that the law does not merely hear but truly *listens*.

References

Arstein-Kerslake, A. (2016). An Empowering Dependency: Exploring Support for the Exercise of Legal Capacity. *Scandinavian Journal of Disability Research, 18*(1), 77–92. https://doi.org/10.1080/15017419.2014.941926

Arstein-Kerslake, A. (2017). Denying Legal Capacity to People with Cognitive Disability. In *Restoring Voice to People with Cognitive Disabilities* (pp. 64–97). https://doi.org/10.1017/9781316493526.007

Devi, N., Bickenbach, J., & Stucki, G. (2011). Moving Towards Substituted or Supported Decision-Making? Article 12 of the Convention on the Rights of Persons with Disabilities. *Alter, 5*(4), 249–264. https://doi.org/10.1016/J.ALTER.2011.07.002

Fallon-Kund, M., Coenen, M., & Bickenbach, J. E. (2017). Balancing Autonomy and Protection: A Qualitative Analysis of Court Hearings Dealing with Protective Measures. *International Journal of Law and Psychiatry, 53*, 69–76. https://doi.org/10.1016/j.ijlp.2017.06.002

Holness, W. (2014). Equal Recognition and Legal Capacity for Persons with Disabilities: Incorporating the Principle of Proportionality. *South African*

Journal on Human Rights, 30(2), 313–344. https://doi.org/10.1080/19962126.2014.11865111

United Nations. (2020). *International Principles and Guidelines on Access to Justice for Persons with Disabilities.* https://www.ohchr.org/sites/default/files/Documents/Issues/Disability/SR_Disability/GoodPractices/Access-to-Justice-EN.pdf

Open Access This chapter is licensed under the terms of the Creative Commons Attribution 4.0 International License (http://creativecommons.org/licenses/by/4.0/), which permits use, sharing, adaptation, distribution and reproduction in any medium or format, as long as you give appropriate credit to the original author(s) and the source, provide a link to the Creative Commons license and indicate if changes were made.

The images or other third party material in this chapter are included in the chapter's Creative Commons license, unless indicated otherwise in a credit line to the material. If material is not included in the chapter's Creative Commons license and your intended use is not permitted by statutory regulation or exceeds the permitted use, you will need to obtain permission directly from the copyright holder.

9

John's Story—Moving Towards Legal Capacity: The Role of Empowerment and Self-Determination

Patrícia Neca

Abstract John, born in 1962, recalls a supportive childhood, academic success, and active social life. After university and family life, he experienced mental health crises but eventually rebuilt his autonomy—living in a group home, leading community activities, and pursuing goals such as writing his autobiography. In 2017, his daughter petitioned regarding financial management, and John requested a longtime friend as his Accompanying Adult. Paradoxically, in 2020, the court granted his friend general representation while affirming John's personal capacity. John's story highlights self-determination and the importance of social inclusion, of resisting stigma, and of maintaining dignity and choice amid legal interventions.

Interview conducted and analysed by Patrícia Neca.

P. Neca (✉)
Observatory on Disability and Human Rights and Interdisciplinary Centre on Gender Studies, Institute of Social and Political Sciences, University of Lisbon, Lisbon, Portugal
e-mail: pneca@iscsp.ulisboa.pt

© The Author(s) 2026
P. Campos Pinto et al. (eds.), *Equal Rights, Equal Voices*, Palgrave Socio-Legal Studies,
https://doi.org/10.1007/978-3-032-05969-7_9

Keywords Legal capacity • Self-determination • Recovery and resilience • Representation (Accompanying Adult)

Early Years

John was born in 1962 in a former Portuguese colony in Africa. He remembered those days, saying, "We used to pick up pomegranates from the ground and peel them". He moved to Portugal at four and lived with his mother, a housewife, and his older sister. His father was a commander in the colonial war (1961–1974)[1] and was absent for long periods. He described a good relationship with all his family members.

He doesn't talk much about his early years at school. However, he shared some good memories from his teenage years, which he recalled with great nostalgia. He was an outstanding student who worked hard both at school and in sports. He had the highest grade in Portuguese, but he was also good at science. Physical activity was also an important aspect of his daily life. His days were filled with activities from the early morning until the end of the day. He fondly remembers the school he attended and speaks about it in a very positive way: "It was a great school that marked me out".

He also recalled his first love affairs—one at 14 and another at 17—and a good relationship with his teachers. Friendships were also one of the most meaningful experiences for him. At least one of his school friendships, from that school time, has lasted until today. Since 2020, John has chosen, before the court, a friend called Alex to help him manage his financial assets. "Lifelong friends", he said.

After finishing secondary school, at the age of 17/18 (around 1979/1980), John explained that he had to do a "preparatory year" in order to go to university. John described this transition as a great change for him. In his own words, it was a "disaster".

[1] In 1961, liberation movements began to emerge in former Portuguese colonies in Africa, such as Angola. Portugal sent troops to fight these movements, starting the colonial war. The war ended in April 1974 with the fall of the dictatorial regime. The long duration of the conflict (1961–1974) and the high number of deaths were decisive in the fall of the dictatorship (1933–1974) and the beginning of democracy in Portugal.

John explained that suddenly he was out of school, at home, studying without teachers, only from books specifically created for that "preparatory year". These books, according to John, were only made available to students a month before the exams. In his view, this was clearly not enough. He felt that the State "did not respected the students (...) because they should provide study materials on time". In his case, once he had the books available, he studied from 7 a.m. to 12 a.m. Despite the difficulties, he managed to obtain good grades. It was, however, at the ages of 17 and 18, during this transition year, that John's "illness began to arrive".

> A lot of study, a lot of effort, a lot of effort. (...) Physical training, I trained every day. (...) gym, irons, swimming pool (...) rowing, in the sea... it was a lot of effort. (...) Other days it was martial arts, judo, with warm-ups afterwards. After that, at some point, there's a burst - a breakdown....

When John accepted to talk about his life in the context of this interview, he began by saying that he didn't want to talk about the negative moments of his life, the ones that made him suffer. His wish was respected, and this chapter reflects the moments that John wanted to share about his life, complemented by the information available in the court decision.

About this time, John briefly explained that he pushed himself too hard and had a breakdown. After a few months off to recover, he went to the university. This was in the early 1980s.

Adulthood

As an outstanding student, John had the freedom to choose his academic path. He had an interest in both the humanities and sciences. He initially enrolled in a physics course; however, after four years, he switched to mathematics, which he successfully completed.

It was at the university that he met his ex-wife, whom he remembers in a very warm and respectful way. "I met her at university, we got married. For many years we were very happy, and that was that. I really appreciated it". After graduating, the couple had two children. John's son was born when he was 29 years old (in 1991), and his daughter was born when he was 31 years old (in 1993).

He mentioned that he got divorced when his children were about 4/5 years old, that is, when he was about 35 years old. The relationship with his children was described as good. One of the things that made him happier was seeing his children growing up healthy and successful.

After finishing the university, John worked as a math teacher. However, he described that period without enthusiasm because he didn't like his job. It was a "very negative experience", he explained. He admits that the relationship with his students (but also with the other teachers) was not easy: "I don't know, I didn't find it easy to make much conversation with them". Although he didn't like it, he worked in the profession for a while and now presents himself as a "retired teacher".

During the interview, John also mentioned that at some point in his life, he had another work experience related to the military field. This was (and still is) his great passion. He explained that he joined the armed forces but that he had to leave after five months. He didn't mention the reasons for that, or the period of his life when this happened. This period was, however, described in a positive way: "they liked me, and I liked them". He admires military personalities, probably inspired by his father's career. His favourite book is "Les Commandos du desert" (1976), from a French author called Jean Bourdier, about a young officer and the special operations he commanded.

Until 2002, he carried on with his usual life. But after turning 40, his illness worsened, and he began to require support, as stated in the court ruling. In our interview, he was very reserved about this period, particularly regarding the diagnosis of an "incurable disease", and about the hospitalisation period, which was one of the saddest moments of his life. Instead, he chose to focus on the positive experiences.

One of those happy moments involved another of John's great passions, a woman called Emma. Sadly, she passed away when he was nearing his 50s. He talks about this woman as if she was still alive: "I love her so much and have so much respect for her (…) I have her photo (…) on my bed against the pillow. (…) I haven't been able to find the right girlfriend since Emma".

Regarding community support, he explained that after leaving the teaching activity—which he highlighted as a "bad experience"—he started "working" at an organisation, which, in contrast, he really liked: "it's a great mental health organisation, it's the best in the country and one of the best in the world". He was passionate about some of the organisation's projects he was part of. For example, in 2016, when he was 54 years old, he was an active member of a mutual support group led by people with mental illness.

John's support organisation focuses on promoting autonomy, self-determination, empowerment, personal recovery and community inclusion. John advocates for the importance of being a good citizen and a holder of rights: "the right to citizenship (…) the right to buy what you want, the right to work (…) the right to study, the right to fight for your life, to earn your bread".

Currently, John lives in a group home,[2] with five other people, run by the same organisation. He didn't mention for how long he had been living there, but he expressed a great satisfaction with this experience. He also likes the neighbourhood where he lives: a "very beautiful area", with gardens, shops, and several shopping areas.

He is currently the spokesman for the residents of the house: "Everyone respects me, everyone likes me, I support them in everything. (…) I was the one who bought the Christmas lights for the residence". However, living in a group home is not always easy, as he explained. Sometimes, he also has to resolve conflicts: "sometimes it's complicated. (…) they're in psychosis, euphoric, euphoric (…) I get there, I stand in the middle (…) And they stop". Respect is another pillar of his life: "I like to respect and be respected".

He also shared his daily routine. On a normal day, he might get up at 9h30 a.m. or 10 a.m. and go to bed at midnight. He stays at home at

[2] Community Home Residence—a stable, medium- to long-term housing solution for people with the experience of mental illness who need autonomy and independence. It is a type of support that promotes individual autonomy, empowerment of residents (through their progressive responsibility for individual and group decisions and goals), promotes residents' participation in the local community, facilitates access to existing resources (commerce, sports, cultural and leisure facilities, local authorities, social services), provides opportunities to diversify and increase social networks (e.g. neighbours and friends) in order to prevent their isolation in the community and contribute to their social integration.

night: "I don't go out at night, it's dangerous". He likes to rest, so he makes sure he gets a good night's sleep, at least eight to nine hours. "I eat well, I sleep well", John explained. A "healthy mind in a healthy body" is a motto that has been with him ever since he was in high school.

He explained that he lives a very active life, with total autonomy, using all the services available in the neighbourhood and in the community, such as pharmacies, shops, and cafés, among others. He also enjoys shopping and has a budget to spend on the food he likes.

> There is always something to do. Sometimes I go to the shopping centre, to the supermarket, to buy food that I use for myself, such as quince paste, coffee, biscuits, bread, … not alcohol (…) Then I walk round the perimeter of the garden. I do that whenever I can. Sometimes I go to the pharmacy to buy medicine.

He also likes to go for a walk with a friend (from the group home), especially in his neighbourhood, which he finds very pleasant: "I live in a very beautiful area". Sometimes, John gives karate lessons to his friend. John learnt karate as a teenager when he was at school (secondary education). Occasionally, John's friend helps him carry his shopping bags. As a reward, John buys him a snack: "a cheeseburger and some crisps". He also enjoys going to a coffee shop in his neighbourhood to buy cigarettes. Despite having different political orientations—John is more centrist and his friend is leftist—they remain good friends.

He firmly states that he doesn't like political parties, politics, or politicians. However, he keeps a close eye on national and international politics. He has a clear position about the ongoing international armed conflicts. He positions himself in the political spectrum at the centre and presents himself as a peaceful person, but very close to the armed forces, defending: "a patriotic military aristocracy in the centre. The centre, it's in the centre, neither fascism nor communism".

Paradoxically, John decided not to vote and hasn't exercised this political right for many years. John's explanation of why he gave up this fundamental right (to vote) is related to stigma. As a citizen and a patriot, his distrust in the political system came from an experience of discrimination, many years ago, on an election day. He felt disrespected, as he explained: "I haven't voted for many years. I don't set foot in the pooling station (...). Once, I was made fun of, I was a teacher, and I never went there again (...) They disrespected me". Another key concern for him was the fight against stigma.

> Because society stigmatises us. Look at him, he's 'crazy, he's crazy' (...) We're not crazy, ... we're sick, we're human beings, we're men and women and we have our rights (...) And we go to universities and hospitals (...). There's a big stigma (...)

John was highly determined and believed that having dreams helps to protect mental health. One of his dreams is to publish a book that has already been written: "In my autobiography I described the two instances in which I pushed myself too hard, ... which led me to burnout, physically ... and studying for exams (...) to prevent young people from having the breakdown that I had".

Initial Petition

John's legal proceedings began in 2017, when John was 55 years old. At that time, he was already a retired teacher. The petition was initiated by John's daughter, under the former law of partial and full guardianship. In 2018, the new Accompanied Adult Scheme was approved (entering into force in February 2019), and all the legal proceedings underway were transferred to the new legislation. John's explanation for the petition was the following: "It comes from fights between my family... my daughter and my son, between my sister (..) 'I want to be John's guardian', then there are clashes. There's a lot of arguing; I don't want to talk about it".

The initial petition aimed for the court to decide partial guardianship, by nominating a support person to manage his financial assets. The main arguments used were that John had schizophrenia, that his clinical situation was irreversible, and that, as a consequence, he was dependent on a third person to manage all his daily activities, including the management of his income and savings.

At that time, John's mother was the person who informally helped him to look after his financial affairs. She passed away recently, just a few years after the court decision in 2020. Regarding his son and daughter, he explained that they meet on special occasions: "family is more for the special times, for Christmas, for the end of the year and for birthdays, baptisms". The court described his family relations as "unstable".

In the first moment, with the help of a court appointed lawyer, John requested the annulment of the proceedings considering them "exaggerated and unnecessary", as mentioned in the court ruling. He denied the veracity of the alleged facts and completely rejected the proposal to appoint a support person. He considered that he did not need help from anyone to manage his life.

Additionally, John claimed that his daughter could not have initiated a process without his consent (Article 141 of the Civil Code). Still, the judge considered the process valid, arguing that it had been submitted under the previous law, which allowed petitions to be submitted without the approval of the beneficiary of the accompanying measures.

To continue with the process, the judge requested additional information, namely a medical examination involving the public prosecutor's office, and heard several witnesses, including John's daughter, ex-wife, and friend Alex. John was also heard, which was mandatory under the new law. He described the day of the hearing, highlighting the importance of dressing formally in order to convey a positive image of himself to the judge:

> I wore a blazer and a tie, I was well dressed, and we talked about my [medical] assessment - whether I could go to court. I was approved, both by them and by the psychiatrist (…) and the judge came (…). I greeted the judge (…) And the judge said: (…) Feel free, you're not a defendant. Tell me about your life and answer my questions (…) And I answered the questions (…) went well, I was confident, it went well. Everything was on average, I'm happy.

Although the judge established a relationship of trust with John, asking him to keep calm and confident, he also admitted that he "was not comfortable", because he did not know what the final decision would be: "In court, I was even a bit scared that (...) they would take my life away".

Regarding the questions raised by the judge, John explained that they were mainly related to money management. For example, checking whether John recognised the money and whether he felt able to manage small or large amounts of money. John admitted that he told to the judge that he didn't feel able to handle transactions such as buying and selling houses without help, but that when it came to day-to-day living, he considered that he was able to manage his money independently.

John's expectations about the court decision were: "I would get Alex [as a support person]". Alex has been his friend since secondary school, and in his view, having him as a support person, would allow John to remain "neutral" and "get on well with both factions" of the family. He also made clear that he was not angry with his daughter (who made the initial petition): "She thought it [the petition] was for my own good".

Court Decision

In 2020, three years after the initial petition, the court decided to restrict John's right to manage his financial and patrimonial affairs. He was 58 years old, and for the first time in his life, he had a support person and stopped having a bank card.

Respecting John's will expressed during the hearing, the judge decided to nominate Alex, John's friend, as his accompanying adult/support person and person of confidence.[3] The judge explained personally the legal decision to John (during the audience), and John expressed that he was "satisfied" with the decision. But in the interview, he expressed that there was only one problem related to the ATM Card:

> I think I could have an ATM card for myself. I've always had a bank card and I've always done well, but not now (...) But this is frustrating, this card

[3] A "person of confidence" is the person chosen by the person in need of mental health care and expressly appointed, with his or her consent, to assist him or her in the exercise of his or her rights, according to the Mental Health Act (Law 35/2023, of 21 July).

> thing, I think it's a right I have that isn't being respected, to have access to my money freely or to a bank account with a limit.

The court considered that, although John had been diagnosed with schizophrenia, the symptoms were in remission with medication. He was considered capable of managing his person and his life. The court ruling also noted that he only needed supervision to take his medication. On the other hand, and despite the fact that John "has adequate knowledge of the money", regarding the management (and knowledge) of his patrimony, the court decision indicated that "the functional impairment from which he suffers (…) makes it difficult for him to manage assets beyond a small amount". Consequently, the final court decision was: "general representation in the management and administration of the property and general management of the property and assets".

The judge considered, however, that John leads an active life and that imposing a "total restriction" on access to financial resources could be counterproductive. So, the final decision was to give him 50 euros a month, after all his bills are paid (accommodation, food and medication). However, during the interview, John mentioned receiving a higher amount than the one decided by the court:

> Alex gives me 200 euros every two weeks (…) he comes to see me at the group home, and we talk (…) How things are going (…) he pays for my mobile phone (…) manages the expenses of the pharmacy (…) Alex has been impeccable.

John said that the amount of money he receives is "enough" because he "doesn't want to waste the money. (…) If God takes me one day, there will be a good amount left for my children". However, the fact that he does not have an ATM card has been described as a challenge because he has to protect the money from being stolen: "I have my money with me, hidden (…) because sometimes they go there, and it disappears (…)".

The judge included, in the court ruling, an excerpt from Gilles Lipovetsky's book *The Era of Emptiness*, prompting a reflection on the individualism that defines contemporary society. In this context, the excerpt highlights the difficulty of maintaining relationships, using the metaphor of living in a desert to illustrate people's inability to connect with one another. However, the judge does not provide the rationale behind selecting this passage.

Comment

This chapter is based on an in-depth biographical interview conducted with John regarding his life trajectory. He warned us, before signing the informed consent, that he wouldn't share the difficult times, the ones that made him suffer. He is a 62-year-old man with a psychosocial disability who was a successful student, graduated from university, had a job, got married, had children, got divorced, and experienced mental health problems, but was able to reconstruct his life, with autonomy and preserving his freedom.

He currently lives in a group home where he is the spokesperson. John leads an active life and participates in his community. His story highlights the importance of community inclusion in personal recovery (San Juan et al., 2021). John cherishes his freedom, and actively pursues his dreams (for example, writing a book telling his story). He has friends, enjoys walking, appreciates his neighbourhood, and frequently visits cafés and shops to buy his favourite foods. Although he likes politics, he stopped voting many years ago because he had an episode on election day where he felt disrespected. So, he has decided not to vote again. He describes with great satisfaction the freedom of being able to carry out every day routines autonomously, such as going to the supermarket or buying tobacco. This autonomy seems to be very important to him.

In 2017, when John was 55, his daughter filed a petition (Regime of the Accompanied Adult) asking the court to consider him incapable of managing his financial affairs. The petition was made probably because John's mother was getting old, and she was the person who informally helped John with his financial issues.

When John realised that the case would not be set aside, as he had initially tried to do, he made his preference clear: he wanted the accompanying adult who would support him—in his financial decisions—to be his long-time friend Alex, rather than his own children. His primary aim was to maintain a positive relationship with all family members, without exception, while remaining "neutral" in the legal proceedings. He described the legal process as a source of family conflict and recalled a family discussion regarding this matter.

In 2020, when John was 58 years old, the court decided to give Alex "general representation" powers over John's financial issues. The court clearly stated that John was a person fully capable of managing his personal life. After the decision, John maintained control over his life, except for financial issues. By choosing his preference, John exercised self-determination: "the right of individuals to have full power over their own lives (…) including freedom of choice, civil rights, independence, and self-direction" (Cook & Jonikas, 2002, p. 88).

It should also be noted that John also mentioned how important it was to have his voice heard in court, a place where he felt "nervous" because of the important decisions that were going to be made about his life, but where he felt respected. He described the way the judge spoke to him in a positive way, trying to make him feel comfortable during the hearing. It is important to highlight that the way the judge addressed him, making an effort to be clear, can be considered a type of procedural accommodation that ensures more effective access to justice, as stated in Article 13. ° (on "Access to Justice") of the Convention on the Rights of Persons with Disabilities.

Another aspect worth highlighting was the careful way in which John presented himself in court. His sister helped him choose a suit and tie to wear to court. In his words, he was very well dressed. He was prepared for the important moment of making a good impression on the judge. John's family has a high socio-economic background in the military field. He has also retired from work (as a teacher), a factor that may be relevant to understand the final court decision of, for example, allowing him access to a small amount of pocket money every two weeks. Overall, John viewed this outcome positively, although he was disappointed with not being granted access to a bank card.

Money management is a fundamental aspect of autonomy, independent living, social participation, and recovery, as it helps individuals maintain control over their lives and improve their overall quality of life. The lack of financial resources, thus, can negatively impact mental well-being (Elbogen et al., 2011). Having access to pocket money to buy personal goods or contribute to his residence has been essential in enhancing the well-being of individuals with mental health experiences (Elbogen et al., 2011). Despite this, the judge restricted John's access to his ATM card, a decision that contradicts the principle that restrictions should be limited to what is necessary. As John suggested, he could have had access to an account with a limited amount of money instead of facing a complete restriction.

The court decision referred to "general representation" (substitute decision-making) rather than "special representation", which is more in line with the concept of supported decision-making. This concept seems to be missing from the court ruling. However, the relationship with his friend Alex was described as open, friendly and flexible. John's friend seems to be helping him to make decisions, rather than making decisions for him and without listening to him.

In light of this, the question arises as to whether it was really necessary to make a general representation decision. It may be that the court could have decided on a less restrictive type of measure and maintained John's access to the bank card. A decision on general representation did not explicitly ensure what kind of support the guardian should provide to the beneficiary to ensure that John's wishes are always respected. This could be a further step towards a law that is more in line with a human rights approach.

References

Cook, J. A., & Jonikas, J. A. (2002). Self-Determination Among Mental Health Consumers/Survivors: Using Lessons from the Past to Guide the Future. *Journal of Disability Policy Studies, 13*(2). https://doi.org/10.1177/104420730201300204 01

Elbogen, E. B., Tiegreen, J., Vaughan, C., & Bradford, D. W. (2011). Money Management, Mental Health, and Psychiatric Disability: A Recovery-Oriented Model for Improving Financial Skills. *Psychiatric Rehabilitation Journal, 34*(3), 223–231. https://doi.org/10.2975/34.3.2011.223.231

San Juan, N. V., Gronholm, P. C., Heslin, M., Lawrence, V., Bain, M., Okuma, A., & Evans-Lacko, S. (2021). Recovery from Severe Mental Health Problems: A Systematic Review of Service User and Informal Caregiver Perspectives. *Frontiers in Psychiatry, 12*, 1–15. https://doi.org/10.3389/fpsyt.2021.712026

Open Access This chapter is licensed under the terms of the Creative Commons Attribution 4.0 International License (http://creativecommons.org/licenses/by/4.0/), which permits use, sharing, adaptation, distribution and reproduction in any medium or format, as long as you give appropriate credit to the original author(s) and the source, provide a link to the Creative Commons license and indicate if changes were made.

The images or other third party material in this chapter are included in the chapter's Creative Commons license, unless indicated otherwise in a credit line to the material. If material is not included in the chapter's Creative Commons license and your intended use is not permitted by statutory regulation or exceeds the permitted use, you will need to obtain permission directly from the copyright holder.

10

Peter's Story: My Vote, My Right—Opportunities and Challenges to Self-Determination Under the New Legal Capacity Regime

Paula Campos Pinto

Abstract Peter, born prematurely and given for adoption at birth, experienced early instability and abuse in an institution before returning to a caring foster home. He attended a special school and later lived in a group home run by a disability organisation. Active, social, and skilled with computers, he works in the mornings, takes part in pottery and theatre workshops, and is a member of a Self-Advocates Group. Peter's case illustrates the complexities involved in achieving legal capacity reform. On one side, this case is an example of good practice in implementing Article 12 of the CRPD, as the court heard his will and preferences and

Interview conducted and analysed by Paula Campos Pinto.

P. Campos Pinto (✉)
Observatory on Disability and Human Rights and Interdisciplinary Centre on Gender Studies, Institute of Social and Political Sciences,,
University of Lisbon, Lisbon, Portugal
e-mail: mppinto@edu.ulisboa.pt

© The Author(s) 2026

P. Campos Pinto et al. (eds.), *Equal Rights, Equal Voices*, Palgrave Socio-Legal Studies,
https://doi.org/10.1007/978-3-032-05969-7_10

preserved his right to vote. On the other side, the decision is also fraught with contradictions: by nominating the group home director as the financial manager of Peter's estate, the court created a potential conflict of interest. As for Peter, he values his independence and dreams of living on his own.

Keywords Supported decision-making • Voting rights • Self-advocacy • Vulnerability

Peter was born in 1993. As a premature baby, he was kept in an incubator for a few weeks and given up for adoption by his parents at birth. When he was finally discharged from the hospital, he was placed with a foster family by the Social Security Adoption Service. The foster mother, a mature woman with two grown-up daughters, lived in a small town on the outskirts of the capital. Peter spent the first years of his childhood with her. He has fond memories of playing in the backyard of the family home, chatting with the foster mother and helping with the household chores.

When Peter was about six years old, the foster mother felt unable to continue caring for him. Without any other family support, Peter was placed in a residential institution 40 km away from home. The institution hosted orphan girls and boys and other children from disruptive families, whose parents were unable to look after them. However, totally excluded from the community (there was even a school inside the facility), rather than offering protection, it was a place of heightened vulnerability for the children it was supposed to care for. While living there, Peter (and other children) suffered sexual abuse from one of the staff members.

When his adoptive mother found out about it, she came to his rescue and took him back. However, to this day, Peter still carries the scars of this trauma and has difficulty talking about his time in the institution, particularly about the abuse he suffered.

Returning home, Peter resumed schooling. He was nine years old by then and had learned how to read and write but was facing increasing trouble with math. Aware of his difficulties, and with the support of the

Social Security services, the foster mother decided to enrol Peter in the nearby special school, run by a non-profit disability service provider association, where Peter followed an adapted, functional curriculum.

The foster mother provided Peter with a caring environment, though not exempt from its own difficulties: money was scarce, and sometimes Social Security transfers, which were targeted to his needs (e.g., to buy assistive devices), ended up being used for other purposes. Ultimately, these incidents led the Social Security Adoption Services to propose that Peter was admitted to the residential care facility of the same disability service provider organisation he had already attended for schooling. Usually, only youngsters aged 16 years and older would be admitted to the residential care facility, so Peter, 12 years old by then, was an exception. His young age compared to other residents, as well as his lively and social nature, earned him everyone's attention and care, from other residents to staff.

At that time, the organisation, in agreement with Social Security and the foster mother, initiated a guardianship process and eventually became responsible for Peter in a child custody decision issued by the court in 2007. During the legal proceedings, Peter was heard in court and agreed to the final decision: guardianship was given to the president of the association. However, he has remained in contact with the foster mother, whom he calls "mum", and continues to visit whenever he can.

When he turned 18 years old, Peter completed compulsory education[1] and was transferred to the then-called Center of Occupational Activities (now Center of Activities and Capacitation for Inclusion, CACI). He remained living in the residential facility of the association, but this never prevented him from joining activities in the community. For instance, under the influence of a staff member, he started attending church regularly, and in 2013, he chose to be baptised and make the confirmation. Before, in 2008, he had already joined the Scouts group in his community. He progressed there from Explorers to Pioneers just two years later. With the Scouts, he has often participated in camps and other

[1] At the time, in Portugal, compulsory education involved only nine years of schooling. Typically, students will finish compulsory education at 14 years old. Yet students with special needs could benefit from extensions that in practice enabled them to stay in school until they reached 18 years old.

recreational activities, such as peddy-papers. In 2009, he even went on a cruise with the Scouts to the island of Madeira and spent a few days camping on the island, hiking, visiting museums and other tourist sites. Peter took a lot of photographs on this trip. He only left the Scouts in 2018, but he keeps in touch with friends from those days and occasionally joins the group in social activities.

At the time of the interview, Peter worked part-time at a nearby Parish Council, four days a week, doing clerical work. Every day, he gets up in the morning, takes a shower and gets dressed, has his breakfast and takes the bus, then the train, and finally walks for about 10 minutes to go to work. He works from Monday to Thursday, just in the mornings, and earns 20€ a week. At lunchtime, he comes back to the association and joins his peers for lunch. Weekday afternoons are spent in the pottery workshop. With his workshop group, Peter produces cups on demand that are sold by the association. At 5 pm, when the working day is over, Peter takes the bus again to go back to the group home where he lives.

At the group home, Peter fulfils his domestic chores duties. Then, a catering company brings dinner, and he eats together with his peers. After dinner, he relaxes watching TV or playing games on the internet.

Weekends are a bit different. Peter is a member of a community theatre group that rehearses every Saturday morning. The group involves 12 people, both persons with and without intellectual disability. Every year, they put together a play that is exhibited in the month of December. Peter feels very close to the group and greatly enjoys this activity.

On Sundays, he likes to go to the city with friends, be on Facebook and Instagram, and colouring books. He also likes to work on the computer and thinks he is really good at it, especially with Excel, Word and PowerPoint. He dreams of getting proper training as an administrative assistant so that he can have "*a real job*" in the future.

Peter is also a member of the Self-Advocates Group. The association where he lives belongs to a large Federation that hosts a national self-advocate group, and Peter is a highly active member of this group. As such, he attends regular meetings to discuss with his peers and participates in activities to advocate for his rights or to raise public awareness about the rights of persons with disabilities. He has also had the chance to take part in a few international projects. In one of those projects, funded by the European Commission, Peter and other members of the Self-Advocates Group went to Strasbourg and spoke to Members of the European Parliament about the rights of persons with disabilities. In the past, he has also participated in trips to Luxembourg and Italy, to meet with similar Self-Advocate groups in these countries.

In 2018, as with many of its other clients, the organisation made a claim under the former guardianship law (*inabilitação/curadoria*) to obtain legal support for the care provided to Peter. Peter was unable to manage money and needed support with medical care and daily living tasks. Three years later, when the court finally ruled, the new law on the Accompanied Adult was already in place, so it was under the new scheme that the court wrote the sentence. According to Peter, the association wanted to protect him, which he finds important.

During the court case, Peter went to a psychiatric hospital in the city for medical assessment (medical expertise). The manager of the group home took him there. Peter remembers that the doctor asked him a lot of questions, mostly about money, to see if he knew the denominations of different bills and how to make change. But Peter could not understand money.

The court session took place online, as we were in the middle of the COVID-19 pandemic. Peter did not feel stressed about being in front of the judge, as he had been in court before during the child custody proceedings. Peter told the judge that he wanted to be able to vote. The judge asked him the name of the prime minister and the name of the president of the Portuguese Republic. Peter proudly told us that he answered all these questions well—he is interested in politics and keeps updated with the news. The judge also asked whether he liked to live in the group home and whether people treated him well there. He responded affirmatively. And he pointed to the judge whom he would like to be his Accompanying Person: the group home manager, whom he has known since he was 12 years old, when he first arrived at the association. In the final decision issued in 2021, the judge granted him both rights.

In general, Peter is happy with his life. He becomes bored only when he has nothing to do. But he quickly finds something to keep him occupied. He is a very social person, and over the years of living with the same service provider, he has made many friends with the staff and clients of the association, both in the group home and at CACI. He enjoys spending time with them, both inside and outside the walls of the organisation. He also gets on well with his colleagues in the Parish Council. He feels well supported by the association, which is important to him.

Peter is quite aware of his difficulties. He recognises that he needs support, particularly in financial matters, and he appears to have complete trust in the organisation and the staff there to support him with his needs. He has developed an emotional attachment to many of the staff at the service provider, particularly the manager of the group home. In this sense, the organisation is like a family to him. For example, if he needs to buy a new pair of shoes, the manager of the home, his Accompanying Person, will take him shopping. Peter will choose the shoes, and she will pay for them. He never carries the debit card with him, but he does get pocket money for small daily expenses.

But even though he recognises that he has support needs, Peter shared that he was taken aback when he heard about the court decision; it was not an easy or pleasant moment for him:

Interviewer	How did you learn about the court decision?
Peter	My Support Person told me. She called me in, and she said: "Look, this is the decision" and she explained it to me. And I was like, "okay"; I accepted it.
Interviewer	Were you happy about the decision? Was that what you were expecting?
Peter	Okay… I was sad; but then… I accepted it. Of course, right there in the moment, it was like a … a kick in the stomach. But it was … okay.
Interviewer	Why do you tell me it was a kick in the stomach?
Peter	Because it was … This was hard, very … I already knew that the decision was going to be this, right? But … things could have been a little … a little different; but, whatever….
Interviewer	What would you have liked to have been different?
Peter	I don't know … Maybe that … that it would give me a little more freedom, or that [it would say]: "You can do this thing, but you can't do this other one". But … it's okay.

Certainly, the court's decision preserved Peter's right to vote, something he had every reason to value. Certainly, too, the organisation provides him the care and support he needs to feel safe and strive for. But he longed for more. When asked about what he would change in his life if he could, the answer came straightforward and simple:

> I would like to live on my own; I would like to have my own place … a place where I can live by myself, or with friends. And I would like, I don't know, … to have my own life. I think … I think that's something that everybody would like.

The Court's Decision

Initiated in 2018 as a guardianship claim, Peter's case was concluded only three years later, when the new Accompanied Adult legislation was already in place. The court decision is an 11-page document in which the court's decision is based on two sets of elements: "the facts found to be established" and the judge's interpretation of the requirements of the new legislation.

In exposing the "facts considered to be proven", the judge resorts to a markedly medical discourse, reproducing Peter's diagnosis, in a lengthy description filled with medical terms:

The beneficiary was diagnosed with a neurodevelopmental intellectual disorder/mild intellectual disability, associated with dysmetria and muscular atrophy of the lower limbs, mild hearing impairment and visual impairment (severe myopia) of prenatal aetiology (foetal alcohol syndrome).

Then, he proceeds to enumerate Peter's abilities and impairments:

- With the support of third parties, he can orient himself in time and space.
- He is unable to memorise recent events.
- He has no notion of the economic value of goods and money.
- He does not perform personal hygiene without supervision.
- He can read and write.

- He can't do calculation.
- He doesn't know what a credit or debit card is.
- He has a cell phone which he uses to make calls, write short messages, and access the internet.
- He exercises the right to vote.

Referring to Peter's judicial hearing, the court asserts that he showed "the ability to develop a coherent and adequate dialogue". Yet, drawing from the medical report issued at Peter's medical examination, the court concludes that:

The consequences of the impairment are important, and in practical terms, Peter's social functioning and autonomy are somewhat, though not completely, impaired, requiring the assistance of a third party in the context of daily life business and asset management, and in acts that are relevant to health and treatment measures.

After establishing these medical facts, the judge moves on to a detailed interpretation of the new legal framework. Here, two main features of the new law are highlighted: first, that, contrary to the former guardianship regime (*interdição*), the new law "makes it possible to order support measures in relation to only a specific area of the life of the beneficiary"; and second, that it "is governed by a principle of necessity". Citing a well-known legal scholar in the country, the court thus concludes that the most appropriate measure in Peter's case is the "special representation" regime, in which the Support Person must assist the beneficiary in managing his assets, particularly in obtaining the pensions/allowances to which he is entitled, in managing bank accounts if necessary, and in fulfilling his obligations, in particular in dealing with state institutions, as well as in deciding on health-related matters (concerning medical care and treatment).

The sentence further establishes a Family Council responsible for monitoring the way in which the Support Person's duties are performed. In Peter's case, the Family Council comprises two persons, who are also staff members of the association he attends.

In determining the duties of the Support Person as well as Peter's rights, the court specifies that the Support Person can substitute Peter in obtaining the social benefits and pensions he is entitled to, but the management of those assets "must be carried out jointly with the beneficiary". Moreover, Peter retains the right to engage in a professional activity, although "he must be assisted in the celebration of employment contracts". Finally, the judge limits Peter's right to test and donate, but she clarifies that Peter "maintains the right to vote".

Comment

Peter's case illustrates the complexities involved in achieving legal capacity reforms (Dinerstein, 2012). On one side, it is an example of good practice in implementing Article 12 of the CRPD—Peter had the chance to express his will and preferences before the court; the court respected his wishes and choices; the support measures ruled by the court address Peter's needs (e.g. his difficulties managing money) but do not go beyond what is needed. In other words, and in accordance with a human rights perspective, the court displays an understanding of personhood as eminently relational (Arstein-Kerslake, 2016), in the sense that it recognises Peter's legal capacity while ensuring that he has access to assistive relationships that enable the full expression of his human agency (Carney, 2017).

Nevertheless, the decision is also fraught with contradictions: by nominating the group home director as the financial manager of Peter's estate, the court creates a potential conflict of interest. While intended to protect Peter from his own diminished capacity to deal with finances, this decision may indeed increase his vulnerability and dependence (Arstein-Kerslake, 2016). Truly, it was Peter who chose his Accompanying Person, but the fact that his personal choice fell on the manager of the group home facility where he lives speaks volumes about the limited social networks of many people with intellectual disability. As in other countries, the new Portuguese legal capacity framework does not offer a solution to these cases because the function of professional supporters is not available, and so there are a large number of directors, managers, and staff of disability service providers who end up also being the supporters of the people they serve. Whereas the will and preference of the supported person should always be unquestionable (Flynn & Arstein-Kerslake, 2014), including in choosing his or her supporter, setting up a pool of professional Accompanying Persons, duly trained and closely monitored by an official authority, would allow disabled people with reduced or non-existent informal networks to escape from such conflicting relations of support.

While this is not possible, Peter keeps longing for a "*life of his own*".

References

Arstein-Kerslake, A. (2016). An Empowering Dependency: Exploring Support for the Exercise of Legal Capacity. *Scandinavian Journal of Disability Research, 18*(1), 77–92. https://doi.org/10.1080/15017419.2014.941926

Carney, T. (2017). Prioritising Supported Decision-Making: Running on Empty or a Basis for Glacial-To-Steady Progress? *Laws, 6*(4), 18. https://doi.org/10.3390/laws6040018

Dinerstein, R. (2012). Implementing Legal Capacity Under Article 12 of the UN Convention on the Rights of Persons with Disabilities: The Difficult Road from Guardianship to Supported Decision-Making. *Human Rights Brief, 19*(2), 8–12.

Flynn, E., & Arstein-Kerslake, A. (2014). Legislating Personhood: Realising the Right to Support in Exercising Legal Capacity. *International Journal of Law in Context, 10*(1), 81–104. https://doi.org/10.1017/S1744552313000384

Open Access This chapter is licensed under the terms of the Creative Commons Attribution 4.0 International License (http://creativecommons.org/licenses/by/4.0/), which permits use, sharing, adaptation, distribution and reproduction in any medium or format, as long as you give appropriate credit to the original author(s) and the source, provide a link to the Creative Commons license and indicate if changes were made.

The images or other third party material in this chapter are included in the chapter's Creative Commons license, unless indicated otherwise in a credit line to the material. If material is not included in the chapter's Creative Commons license and your intended use is not permitted by statutory regulation or exceeds the permitted use, you will need to obtain permission directly from the copyright holder.

11

Conclusion: Legal Capacity and the CRPD—Voices, Contexts and Lessons for Future Legal Reform

Paula Campos Pinto, Teresa Janela Pinto, Patrícia Neca, and Fernando Fontes

Abstract The conclusion examines how legal regimes continue to limit adults with disabilities despite the CRPD promises. Using data from the EQUAL project, particularly the six life stories, it contrasts international norms affirming equal legal capacity with persistent substituted decision-making in practice. From the voices and experiences of the case studies presented, several common and interrelated themes are identified, allowing for a more comprehensive understanding of the factors that enable or obstruct disability justice. The authors argue that law reform alone cannot ensure autonomy; cultural norms, institutional practices, and scarce

P. Campos Pinto (✉) • T. J. Pinto • P. Neca
Observatory on Disability and Human Rights and Interdisciplinary Centre on Gender Studies, Institute of Social and Political Sciences, University of Lisbon, Lisbon, Portugal
e-mail: mppinto@edu.ulisboa.pt; teresajpinto@iscsp.ulisboa.pt; pneca@iscsp.ulisboa.pt

F. Fontes
Centro de Estudos Sociais, University of Coimbra, Coimbra, Portugal
e-mail: fernandofontes@ces.uc.pt

© The Author(s) 2026

P. Campos Pinto et al. (eds.), *Equal Rights, Equal Voices*, Palgrave Socio-Legal Studies,
https://doi.org/10.1007/978-3-032-05969-7_11

community support services undermine rights on the ground. They call for a comprehensive implementation of legal reform, training of staff, monitoring, and resources to transform a formal reform into people's everyday inclusion and dignity.

Keywords UNCRPD (Article 12) • Legal capacity • Guardianship reform • Autonomy and self-determination • Portugal case study

Oscar, Mary, Samuel, Sophie, John, and Peter are adults with intellectual or psychosocial disabilities who have had their legal capacity revoked or limited. Like many others around the world, their life stories speak volumes about the barriers and obstacles that many people with disabilities continue to face in achieving full citizenship (Kymlicka & Donaldson, 2017) as well as about their struggles and successes in affirming human dignity and rights.

The Convention on the Rights of Persons with Disabilities introduced a paradigm shift in the way disability is understood and addressed in society and by law (Mégret, 2008). A particularly transformative feature of the treaty is the recognition of legal capacity and equality before the law for people with disabilities without exception. Article 12 asserts that *all* persons with disabilities have full legal capacity *everywhere* and cannot be deprived or limited in this right on an unequal basis with other citizens. It also states that States Parties shall ensure that appropriate measures are in place to assist persons with disabilities in the exercise of their legal capacity.

However, the international literature shows that although many countries have introduced legislation on support mechanisms, there has been limited success in abolishing substitute decision-making (Glen, 2015; Martinez-Pujalte, 2019). Courts tend to follow old habits when assessing capacity and attempts at reform to revoke guardianship have generally not been successful (Quinn, 2010).

This book set out to explore tensions arising between the human rights norms and principles laid out in Article 12 of the CRPD, legal frameworks in place at domestic level and the social contexts surrounding the daily lives of persons with intellectual and or psychosocial disabilities. It draws from the results of the EQUAL project, a large study that examined the conditions of implementation of the legal capacity reform initiated in Portugal following the ratification of the CRPD. The new Accompanied Adult Regime (Law 49/2018) replaced the more rigid and paternalistic institute of guardianship (*interdição*, a form of substituted decision-making). Shifting towards the principle of *protecting without incapacitating*, at least in theory, the new scheme emphasises self-determination and the provision of support rather than the removal of rights. It also introduces a more flexible, individualised approach that allows persons to participate in legal decisions, appoint their supporters (the so-called *accompanying persons*), and request the periodic revision of support measures—bringing Portuguese law closer to the standards set out in Article 12 of the CRPD (Cordeiro, 2018).

The EQUAL study involved an analysis of 747 court decisions under the Accompanied Adult Regime, 31 semi-structured interviews with key stakeholders, four focus groups with 19 people directly affected by the law, and six case studies with persons with intellectual or psychosocial disabilities who have had their legal capacity restricted or removed. Although the book mainly draws from research conducted in Portugal, the first chapter by Eilionóir Flynn outlined the requirements of Article 12 and provided a review of several legal capacity regimes, drawing lessons for legal reform efforts across the globe that grant the right to enjoy legal capacity, not just in Portugal but internationally.

Adopting a sociolegal analytical lens that integrates the conceptual and theoretical tools of Human Rights Theory and the emerging field of the Sociology of Human Rights (Frezzo, 2015; Pinto, 2023), this concluding chapter synthesises the book's main arguments to underscore the persistent challenges in achieving legal capacity reform aligned with Article 12 of the CRPD. It also offers key lessons and recommendations aimed at advancing equality, self-determination, and full citizenship for persons with disabilities in contemporary societies.

Cross-Cutting Themes

The autobiographical narratives of the men and women interviewed for the case studies shaped and informed our analytical approach. These life stories offer sociological portraits (Lahire, 2002) that illuminate the social, economic, cultural, and political forces that have shaped individual trajectories over time. At the same time, they foreground individual agency, even in contexts in which resources to pursue one's will and aspirations were limited or absent. From their voices and experiences, several common and interrelated themes emerged, allowing for a more comprehensive understanding of the factors that enable or obstruct disability justice. We explore these themes below, integrating data from the other strands of the EQUAL project into this final discussion.

The Continuing Centrality of the Medical Model and Medical Discourses

The continued dominance of the medical model of disability poses a significant barrier to the effective implementation of legal capacity reforms. Although in Portugal, as in many other countries, recent legislative developments have moved towards a human rights-based framework, the case studies of Sophie, Oscar, Peter, and Mary reveal how medicalised understandings—centred on diagnosis, impairment, and vulnerability—remain deeply embedded in judicial reasoning. It has been noted that legal actors frequently treat diagnostic categories as proxies for capacity, reproducing outdated assumptions and failing to recognise disability as socially constructed (Arstein-Kerslake, 2017). Surely, in Portugal, some judicial decisions have become less severe over time (as presented in Chap. 4), but the enduring focus on clinical assessments continues to undermine the reform's transformative potential (Krieger, 2003). This is illustrated by the impressively wide range of medical diagnoses used to support the 747 court rulings examined in the EQUAL project. In many of them (54.5%), apart from mentioning either very specific (e.g. "Metachromatic Leukodystrophy") or vague (e.g. "Developmental Disorder") or even outdated terms (e.g. "Deaf-Mute"), there is a lack of detail about what such diagnoses entail. And yet these obscure medical labels are the grounds on which rights are withdrawn and measures of protection and control enforced (Foucault, 1976).

In Mary's case, which was still judged under the previous guardianship regime, the court relied on a medical assessment that invoked IQ test scores and the outdated term "feeble mind" to characterise her as having a "very high cognitive dysfunction" reinforcing a pathologising view of her capacity. A similar legal discourse, grounded in medical diagnosis, remains prevalent in certain court decisions issued under the new law. In Peter, Oscar, and Sophie's cases, for example, the court rulings include an extensive reproduction of their clinical diagnoses, followed by a detailed inventory of areas in which their functioning is deemed compromised, while disregarding the activities they can perform either independently or with minimal support. This was especially striking in Sophie's court documents, which overlooked the positive elements of the initial petition and focused exclusively on areas of deficit and diminished autonomy.

These medical assessments result in negative and totalising judgements about people's abilities. Sophie is deemed "entirely incapable of surviving without the permanent support of another person" while Oscar's sentence concludes that he is "permanently incapable of self-determination regarding the fulfilment of his duties or the exercise of his personal and property rights". These findings echo Arstein-Kerslake's (2017) critique of the medical model, which reduces people to diagnostic labels and neglects their broader social contexts.

The Persistence of the "capacity contract"

Linked to the first, a second key theme is the enduring influence of the capacity contract (Clifford, 2014; Simplican, 2015)—a normative framework that ties political and legal personhood to the possession of a threshold level of rational capacity. The capacity contract enshrines cognitive competence as a prerequisite for full citizenship, systematically excluding those deemed incapable of reasoning or self-governance. Oscar and Mary's court rulings emphasise their inability to think rationally and apply self-control. Oscar is described as having "bouts of heteroagressiveness that are difficult to control" and an "inability to adapt to any training or activity". Mary is said to "reveal ideoinstinctive thinking, with little planning and without analysing the consequences and implications of her actions".

While presented as a safeguard for political and legal legitimacy, the capacity contract operates as a mechanism of domination, justifying the withdrawal of rights and reinforcing unequal power relations. Oscar's court decision led to severe curtailing of personal rights, preventing him from travelling independently beyond the confines of the institution where he resides. Mary's daily routine is organised (and thus also controlled) by the local disability service provider organisation she attends. This reflects a trend to conflate legal capacity with mental capacity in legal practice (Barton-Hanson, 2018; de Bhailís & Flynn, 2017). By privileging control, protection, and conformity over autonomy and self-determination, the capacity contract sustains paternalistic legal practices and perpetuates the structural exclusion of disabled people from full citizenship (Kymlicka & Donaldson, 2017) and equal participation in the justice system. As a result, substituted decision-making continues to prevail over supported decision-making. Rather than empowering individuals, the system assumes that a representative or someone else must decide what is best on their behalf.

The supported decision-making model advanced by the CRPD, on the contrary, promotes an expanded conception of autonomy and decision-making—not as fixed traits, but as relational and dynamic processes, shaped by an individual's context, support networks, and broader social and institutional environments (Arstein-Kerslake, 2016; Fallon-Kund et al., 2017). Certainly, as detailed on Chap. 3, the Portuguese legal framework now formally endorses the principle of flexible, individualised support—described by one of our interviewees as akin to a "tailor-made suit"—yet this approach remains inconsistently applied in practice. As our assessment of court rulings under the new law evidenced (see Chap. 4), courts often revert to standardised procedures and binary assessments, which ultimately constrain the law's capacity to facilitate truly person-centred decision-making.

Lack of Procedural Accommodations

Human rights are "indivisible, and interdependent and interrelated" (United Nations, 1993). Among others, Article 12 must be read in conjunction with Article 13 of the CRPD (Access to Justice), which mentions the right to procedural accommodations. These include "all necessary and appropriate modifications and adjustments in the context of access to justice, where needed in a particular case, to ensure the participation of persons with disabilities on an equal basis with others" (United Nations, 2020). The lack of these provisions undermines the inclusive aims of legal capacity reforms. During the hearing, Peter expressed the importance of the right to vote; John indicated whom he wanted to be his supporter (a friend rather than a family member). Both were heard by the judge in court, and their will and preferences were respected. John said he was "satisfied" with the court's decision. On the contrary, Oscar complained that the judge did not give him time to think before answering: "They started bombarding me, several things in a row (…). And I blocked it. I couldn't say anything more". This description suggests that the judge did not adjust nor provide any accommodation to ensure that Oscar was given the opportunity to express himself on an equal basis with others. As for Sophie's right to be heard, it was simply denied: neither the public defender nor the judge ever met or heard Sophie or her family, effectively disregarding her right to a direct hearing.

The provision of accommodations in legal proceedings ensures meaningful participation of the person with disabilities (Neca, 2023), but it also enables judicial officers to achieve a more thorough understanding of the abilities and support needs of that individual. It may, however, require additional resources, whether human (for instance, if Sign Language Interpreters or other communication facilitators are needed) or time resources. As explained by one of our interviewees, this conflicts with New Public Management models (Hood, 1991) currently imposed on Portuguese courts which demand that legal proceedings are conducted "faster, faster, and faster" when "this law is inherently slower!" (B4 Expert). As the cases of Oscar and Sophie illustrate, the tensions and paradoxes emerging from these opposing forces often lead to a lack of provision of procedural accommodations that ultimately prevent the active participation of persons with disabilities in decisions that profoundly affect their lives.

The "capture of the new law"

The tendency of legal decisions under the new legal capacity law to reproduce features of the old guardianship regime signals the courts' difficulty in fully embracing the intended paradigm shift and may suggest a "capture of the new law" (Krieger, 2003), another cross-cutting theme identified in our analysis. While Law 49/2018 was conceived as a transformative reform aligned with the CRPD, aimed at redefining legal capacity and promoting rights-based support models, its implementation has been inconsistent and, in many cases, curtailed. This gap between legal promise and practice is evident in most of the case studies, despite a few more positive examples, such as those of Peter and John.

The quantitative analysis of the 747 court sentences issued in three judicial districts in Portugal during the first four years of the implementation of the new Adult Accompanied Regime reveals a systematic reliance on general (82.5%) rather than special representation (16.5%), along with a tendency to impose restrictions on rights, including personal rights, beyond what is required or justified (with 90% of the cases withdrawing at least one personal right, but up to 11 personal rights). The cases of Oscar, Mary, Samuel, Sophie, and John clearly illustrate this form of constraint in the application of the new legal regime.

Oscar's case is archetypal of how the spirit of the new law and the CRPD can be distorted, particularly through the central role assigned to disability service provider organisations and the transfer of power into the hands of the directors of these organisations—at the expense of preserving disabled people's legal capacity. As our analysis showed, the judge in Oscar's case opted for the application of general representation and appointed the president of the disability service provider institution he attends as his supporter and legal representative. Interviews with key stakeholders analysed in Chap. 4 further revealed that the appointment by the court of a representative of the disability service provider as a support person is a recurrent practice when the person with disabilities lacks an informal social network. This practice, however, complicates power dynamics, creates potential conflicts of interest and limits the space for the person's autonomous decision-making.

The new law has been captured also by not taking advantage of its full potential. Mary and Samuel's cases, both ruled under the previous legal capacity law, have never been revisited - despite the 2018 reform establishing that support measures must be reviewed whenever necessary and, at a minimum, every five years. The new law has had no tangible impact in either case, but this failure to act illustrates a broader pattern of inertia that also undermines the effect of legal reform.

These examples are not exhaustive of the various ways in which the new regime's implementation has been limited, or its core ideas and objectives have been diluted. They also do not account for broader structural challenges, such as limited judicial resources and a lack of community-based support services, which further hinder the law's consistent and meaningful application.

The "capture" of the new regime is largely due to the fact that, as Krieger puts it, "law does not exercise a direct effect on individuals. [...] formal law is filtered through (...) mediating norms and institutions, it is interpreted, constituted, and reenacted in ways that tend to reflect and reify them" (2003, p. 348). In the case of the new legal capacity law, this outcome reflects the convergence of several factors. Chief among them is the top-down nature of the reform, which has clashed with deeply entrenched institutions and dominant value systems operating in various social spheres, including the justice system and its officials. Moreover, this transition has not been driven or sustained by a strong disability rights movement advocating and pushing for change in this area. Notably, people with intellectual disabilities have remained largely absent from the Portuguese disability movement, and their views, needs, and demands have often been marginal within the movement's agenda (Fontes, 2014, 2016).

Multiple Intersecting Systems of Oppression

The lives of persons with intellectual and psychosocial disabilities are entangled in *multiple intersecting systems of oppression* that exacerbate their social exclusion, economic exploitation, stigma, and social devaluation—and this has emerged as another cross-cutting theme in our analysis. Law and legal decisions are an important element in the more complex reality of "structural ableism", which Lundberg & Chen (2023, p. 1) have defined as

> a system of historical and contemporary policies, institutions, and societal norms and practices that devalue and disadvantage people who are disabled, neurodivergent, chronically ill, mad, and/or living with mental illness and privilege people who are positioned as able-bodied and able-minded.

Court decisions that remove or limit legal capacity have a profound impact on everyday lives, not just because they withdraw fundamental rights, but because they produce a sense of powerlessness and diminished human dignity and worth: Peter experiences a "*k*ick in the stomach" when he hears the sentence; Oscar feels discriminated against and wants "his life back"; Mary bursts into tears when she speaks about her son whom the court has removed from her; and Samuel, with a lifelong experience of discredit and distrust, learned that silence is the best way to protect himself from the symbolic violence he has faced. Describing how the entire process that led to his interdiction was "kept secret", he confided feeling sad and disappointed and to date does not understand the reasons behind the decision.

Structural ableism has a particularly detrimental impact on persons with disabilities who live at the intersection of multiple systems of oppression (Lundberg & Chen, 2023), such as those based on socio-economic status, gender, race, age, migrant status, geographic location, and other markers of identity. In capitalist societies, naturally, class plays a key role in upholding discrimination. Studies have pointed out that persons with disabilities live disproportionately below the poverty line (Berie et al., 2024) and that poverty and deprivation shape the impairment experience throughout the life cycle, increasing the barriers and reducing the opportunities for full development (Galea-Curmi, 2023). John's financial power, as demonstrated by his careful choice of a "nice suit" to wear to court, where he eventually obtained a more favourable decision, is a clear indication that money matters when it comes to the presentation of the self (including a disabled self) in the world. Likewise, Sophie's family's ability to continue to provide conditions for a satisfying and independent life, even in the face of a very restrictive court ruling, sharply contrasts with Oscar, Mary, or Samuel's experiences, whose lives, marked by poverty and economic deprivation, seem to be more deeply imprisoned by the similarly harsh court decisions imposed on them.

One of the effects of structural ableism is denying or restricting access to resources (Lundberg & Chen, 2023) which increases social vulnerability and produces new tensions and contradictions. Such a paradox becomes apparent in rulings that remove rights and promote substitutes, as opposed to supported decision-making regimes, in order to protect people deemed more vulnerable due to their cognitive or mental health characteristics, while their biographic narratives expose the processes of vulnerability to which those same people are subjected to when their legal capacity rights are withdrawn or limited (Arstein-Kerslake, 2016). For example, Oscar, Mary, and, until recently, Peter, as well as several of the focus group participants, carry out the so-called socially useful activities in the community on a daily basis. Although these activities are subject to a fixed and regular schedule (which can vary from two to four days per week) and involve tasks with some degree of difficulty, the remuneration they receive in return is insignificant, always below €100/month, and excludes any form of social benefit, amounting to a form of economic exploitation.

Informal restrictions on people's freedom to make decisions about their lives often compound legal measures to limit or remove their legal capacity. Through an informal agreement between Mary's family and the disability service provider she attends, Mary is now under the responsibility of the organisation. Every day, Mary goes to and from work on the private bus of the institution, which is convenient for her since she lives in a rural area where transportation systems are deficient, but also becomes a subtle way of controlling her whereabouts. This is largely due to persisting paternalistic and stigmatising views of disability, which shape society's attitudes towards persons with intellectual and psychosocial disabilities and impact their well-being and ability to exert self-determination. With the exception of asset management, an area where he acknowledges that he needs support, John has been able to retain his rights but still struggles with the stigma of mental illness. As for Peter, despite receiving a less restrictive sentence, and having had a say in the choice of his supporter, he continues to long for a home and a life "of his own", suggesting that his ability to make choices about his life may be more compromised than he describes.

Moreover, sentences handed down before the entry into force of Law 49/2018 (i.e. before 10 February 2019) may (and should) be reviewed at the request of the accompanied adult, the accompanying person, or the Public Prosecutor's Office. Yet, neither Mary's nor Samuel's sentences, ruled under the old guardianship institute (*interdição*), have yet been reviewed, and there appear to be no plans for such a review. These cases further illustrate how disempowered persons with disabilities lack support systems to assist them in claiming legal capacity. As a result, disparities in the application of legal norms within the same country may further their exclusion and de-citizenship status (Devlin & Pothier, 2006).

In short, by naming structural ableism, we not only challenge the individual and medical model that still dominates society's understanding of and response to disability, but also expose the complex interplay of systems of oppression that operate to perpetuate disability discrimination, inequality, and injustice, including enjoying legal capacity.

Increasing Awareness of Rights

Despite these obstacles, there appears to be a shift towards greater awareness of the CRPD's legal capacity provisions among judicial officers, families, and directors of disability service provider organisations, as well as among persons with disabilities. This is evident in the evolving patterns of court rulings during the first four years of implementation of the legal reform in Portugal, which have gradually shifted towards less restrictive forms of support. This is also evident in the overwhelming recognition and appreciation of the progressive features of the new law expressed by our interviewees. Above all, this is evident in the self-advocacy efforts of people with intellectual and psychosocial disabilities. This growing awareness suggests that a fundamental cultural shift is underway, but it also highlights the ongoing need to align legal frameworks and support systems with the principles of dignity, inclusion, and autonomy, as outlined in the CRPD.

Lessons Learned and the Way Forward

As our results highlight, in Portugal, legal improvement regarding disabled people's legal capacity, both in terms of legal standing and legal agency, endorsed by Law 49/2018 of 14 August, originated in external, top-down, decisions, rather than in internal and organic movements and/or demands. Moreover, research results revealed the devastating consequences for those people under the previous institutes of guardianship and curatorship, prevented from exercising civil and political rights, and the promises of the new legal regime, of the *Accompanied Adult*, to end this "civil death". Despite being adamant in preserving people's legal capacity, the new legal scheme enacted is still struggling to impose the needed social and legal paradigm shift. This fact reveals the constructed nature of legal capacity and of law and of law application as a terrain of materialisation of formal and informal social norms (Krieger, 2003). Rather than being a static and an individual domain, decision-making capacity emerges as a relational, dynamic, and interconnected (Arstein-Kerslake, 2016; Fallon-Kund et al., 2017), and legal capacity as a social and political construct, geographically and historically situated.

To move forward, a number of gaps, tensions, and contradictions need to be addressed. The lack of resources has been identified, by those in the field, as one of the main difficulties, compromising the process of legal change and the impact of the changes being introduced. In order to bring about far-reaching change, the resources and responsiveness of the justice system and community support services need to be strengthened.

Human resources are pivotal to the implementation of the new legal regime, as any solution needs to be built with and, always, hearing persons with disabilities, needs to respect their voices, will, and aspirations, and needs to preserve their legal capacity. The complexity of legal capacity processes requires the establishment of multidisciplinary teams, composed of professionals from legal and social backgrounds as well as peer support, to facilitate dealing with the diversity of life experiences, communication styles, and support needs of persons with impairments. Adequate human and time resources should be allocated to enable these teams to intervene at different stages of legal capacity proceedings (from the development of the initial claim to the hearing and post-sentence follow-up).

Transformative law is a tool for social change, "designed to subvert and reconstruct relevant institutionalized categories, it may also be deployed to displace institutionalized patterns of inference and action" (Krieger, 2003, p. 345). As such, transformative law may be considered a threat to dominant social consensus, originating pockets of resistance where new norms and values clash with dominant social norms and institutions. Several forms of resistance capturing the new law were identified, and they require thoughtful consideration. A form of subversion of the embedded spirit of the new regime is the preservation of the traditional central role of disability professionals and of disability service providers in disabled people's lives, especially in the lives of people with intellectual and psychosocial impairments. This has been mirrored by the designation of disability professionals and directors of these service providers as disabled people's support persons under the new Accompanied Adult Regime. In order to prevent dependence, abuse of power and influence, and promote persons with disabilities' independence, we, thus, suggest the creation of a pool of professionals, duly trained and monitored, who can ensure support for people without an identified informal support network.

Challenging and displacing the dominant consensus also requires the dissemination of new values and ideas to reduce resistance and create space for critical thinking. In terms of legal capacity reform, given the revolutionary and paradigmatic change it implies, it is therefore of paramount importance to promote training on disability from a human rights perspective and on the provisions enshrined in the CRPD. This includes educating persons with intellectual and psychosocial disabilities about their rights and responsibilities as citizens in order to empower them, as well as strengthening the training and promoting the transformation of services and support structures for persons with disabilities from a human rights perspective.

In addition, the social, cultural, political, and legal changes envisaged by any reform of legal capacity require continuous monitoring of the application of new legislation, including a thorough assessment of its impact on the living experiences of persons with disabilities.

References

Arstein-Kerslake, A. (2016). An Empowering Dependency: Exploring Support for the Exercise of Legal Capacity. *Scandinavian Journal of Disability Research, 18*(1), 77–92. https://doi.org/10.1080/15017419.2014.941926

Arstein-Kerslake, A. (2017). Denying Legal Capacity to People with Cognitive Disability. In *Restoring Voice to People with Cognitive Disabilities* (pp. 64–97). Cambridge University Press. https://doi.org/10.1017/9781316493526.007

Barton-Hanson, R. (2018). Reforming Best Interests: The Road Towards Supported Decision-Making. *Journal of Social Welfare and Family Law, 40*(3), 277–298. https://doi.org/10.1080/09649069.2018.1493650

Berie, T., Kidd, S. A., & Wolbring, G. (2024). Poverty (Number 1 Goal of the SDG) of Disabled People Through Disability Studies and Ability Studies Lenses: A Scoping Review. *Sustainability, 16*(13), 5814. https://doi.org/10.3390/SU16135814

Clifford, S. (2014). Politics, Groups, and Identities the Capacity Contract: Locke, Disability, and the Political Exclusion of "Idiots". *Politics, Groups, and Identities, 2*, 90–103. https://doi.org/10.1080/21565503.2013.876918

Cordeiro, A. M. (2018). Da situação jurídica do maior acompanhado. Estudo de política legislativa relativo a um novo regime das denominadas incapacidades dos maiores. *Revista de Direito Civil, Ano, III*, 473–554.

de Bhailís, C., & Flynn, E. (2017). Recognising Legal Capacity: Commentary and Analysis of Article 12 CRPD. *International Journal of Law in Context, 13*(1), 6–21. https://doi.org/10.1017/S174455231600046X

Devlin, R., & Pothier, D. (2006). Introduction: Toward a Critical Theory of Dis-Citizenship. In D. Pothier & R. Devlin (Eds.), *Critical Disability Theory: Essays in Philosophy, Politics, Policy, and Law* (pp. 1–22). UBC Press.

Fallon-Kund, M., Coenen, M., & Bickenbach, J. E. (2017). Balancing Autonomy and Protection: A Qualitative Analysis of Court Hearings Dealing with Protective Measures. *International Journal of Law and Psychiatry, 53*, 69–76. https://doi.org/10.1016/j.ijlp.2017.06.002

Fontes, F. (2014). The Portuguese Disabled People's Movement: Development, Demands and Outcomes. *Disability & Society, 29*(9), 1398–1411. https://doi.org/10.1080/09687599.2014.934442

Fontes, F. (2016). *Pessoas com deficiência em Portugal*. Fundação Francisco Manuel dos Santos.

Foucault, M. (1976). *Histoire de la Folie à l'Âge Classique*. Gallimard.

Frezzo, M. (2015). *The Sociology of Human Rights*. Polity Press.

Galea-Curmi, E. (2023). Poverty, Deprivation and Disabled Children's Right to Citizenship. In A. Beckett & A. M. Callus (Eds.), *The Routledge International Handbook of Children's Rights and Disability* (pp. 129–146). Taylor-Francis.

Glen, K. B. (2015). Supported Decision-Making and the Human Right of Legal Capacity. *INCLUSION, 3*(1), 2–16. https://doi.org/10.1352/2326-6988-3.1.2

Hood, C. (1991). A Public Management for All Seasons? *Public Administration, 69*(1), 3–19. https://doi.org/10.1111/J.1467-9299.1991.TB00779.X

Krieger, L. H. (2003). Sociolegal Backlash. In L. H. Krieger (Ed.), *Backlash Against the ADA: Reinterpreting Disability Rights* (pp. 340–393). The University of Michigan Press.

Kymlicka, W., & Donaldson, S. (2017). Inclusive Citizenship Beyond the Capacity Contract. In A. Shachar, R. Buabock, I. Bloemraad, & M. Vink (Eds.), *The Oxford Handbook of Citizenship* (pp. 838–860). Oxford University Press.

Lahire, B. (2002). *Portraits sociologiques: Dispositions et variations individuelles*. Nathan.

Lundberg, D. J., & Chen, J. A. (2023). Structural Ableism in Public Health and Healthcare: A Definition and Conceptual Framework. *The Lancet Regional Health - Americas, 30*(100650), 1–8. https://doi.org/10.1016/J.LANA.2023.100650

Martinez-Pujalte, A. (2019). Legal Capacity and Supported Decision-Making: Lessons from Some Recent Legal Reforms. *Laws, 8*(1), 4. https://doi.org/10.3390/LAWS8010004

Mégret, F. (2008). The Disabilities Convention: Towards a Holistic Concept of Rights. *The International Journal of Human Rights, 12*(2), 261–278. https://doi.org/10.1080/13642980801954363

Neca, P. (2023). *Briefing Paper on Barriers Faced by Defendants with Intellectual and/or Psychosocial Disabilities in the Criminal Justice System in Portugal.*
Pinto, P. C. (2023). Disability and Human Rights. In R. L. Brown, M. Maroto, & D. Pettinicchio (Eds.), *The Oxford Handbook of the Sociology of Human Rights* (pp. 175–194). Oxford University Press.
Quinn, G. (2010). Personhood & Legal Capacity: Perspectives on the Paradigm Shift of Article 12. *Paper Presented at the HPOD Conference, February 2010.*
Simplican, S. C. (2015). *The Capacity Contract: Intellectual Disability and the Question of Citizenship.* University of Minnesota Press.
United Nations. (1993). *Vienna Declaration and Programme of Action (UN Doc. A/CONF.157/24).* https://www.ohchr.org/en/instruments-mechanisms/instruments/vienna-declaration-and-programme-action
United Nations. (2020). *International Principles and Guidelines on Access to Justice for Persons with Disabilities.* https://www.ohchr.org/sites/default/files/Documents/Issues/Disability/SR_Disability/GoodPractices/Access-to-Justice-EN.pdf

Open Access This chapter is licensed under the terms of the Creative Commons Attribution 4.0 International License (http://creativecommons.org/licenses/by/4.0/), which permits use, sharing, adaptation, distribution and reproduction in any medium or format, as long as you give appropriate credit to the original author(s) and the source, provide a link to the Creative Commons license and indicate if changes were made.

The images or other third party material in this chapter are included in the chapter's Creative Commons license, unless indicated otherwise in a credit line to the material. If material is not included in the chapter's Creative Commons license and your intended use is not permitted by statutory regulation or exceeds the permitted use, you will need to obtain permission directly from the copyright holder.

FSC
www.fsc.org
MIX
Papier | Fördert
gute Waldnutzung
FSC® C083411

Kolibri 360 GmbH
Ferdinand-Jühlke-Straße 7
99095 Erfurt, Deutschland
produktsicherheit@kolibri360.de